LETTERS OF HADRAT UMAR FAROOQ

(R.A.A.)

Translated by

Dr. Hafiz Muhammad Adil
M.A., LL.B., Ph.D.

KITAB BHAVAN
New Delhi-110002

KITAB BHAVAN
Exporters & Importers
1784, Kalan Mahal, Daryaganj
New Delhi-110002 [India]
Phones : 3274686, 3263383
Telex : 31-63106 ALI IN

ISBN 81-7151-145-7

First Published in India 1992
2nd Edition : 2008

Published by:
Nusrat Ali Nasri for Kitab Bhavan
1784, Kalan Mahal, Daryaganj
New Delhi-110002 [India]

Printed in India at:
Nazia Printers
Rodgran, Lal Kuan
Delhi-110006

LETTERS OF
HADRAT 'UMAR FAROOQ (R.A.A.)

CONTENTS

* * * * * *

1

بسم الله الرحمن الرحيم

LETTERS OF HADRAT 'UMAR FAROOQ (R.A.A.)

INTRODUCTION

The letters addressed to different officials of the Islamic State by Hadrat 'Umar Farooq (R.A.A.) reflect the working of managing the affairs of different groupings based on ethnic linguistic tendences through the linking forces of Islam. This policy is in continuation of the strategy applied by his predecessors Hadrat Abu Bakr Siddiq (R.A.A.) and the Holy Prophet and Messenger of Allah (S.A.W). As can be seen through the pages of history, in a few years after Hijrat, the Prophet of Allah (S.A.W.) carried the message of Islam in the far off distant corners of Arabian Peninsula and thus laid the foundations of Islamic State as enunciated in the Quran. The establishment of the infant State at Madina was a living practical demonstration of the Quranic theory of life and its administration. At the time of passing of the Prophet of Allah, Muhammad (S.A.W.) from this mundane world, the process of intellectual awakening was at the initial stage. The Meesaq-i-Madina or the Charter of Madina represents the ideal working of managing the affairs of different peoples of different caste, colour, creed and language. But the demise of the Prophet of Allah (S.A.W.) seemed to be the bursting of the lava from a volcano. A considerable populace of Arabia became hostile to the newly established way of life — Deen-e-Islam, as it had not gone deep into the very core of their hearts. The old habits forming part of their second nature, were being revived. On the 12th Rabi-ul-Awwal, 11 A.H. Abu Bakr (R.A.A.) was elected the Caliph or lieutenant of the Messenger of Allah (S.A.W.) certainly against his wishes. The situation was extremely critical. There was potent danger to the newly established ideological infant

State of Madina. Almighty Allah helped the Muslims and the personality of Hadrat Abu Bakr (R.A.A.) was brought in the lime light. It was characteristic of him to show greater resoluteness and determination according to the danger and impending perils. Soon after becoming the Caliph or the true lieutenant of the Messenger of Allah (S.A.W.), Abu Bakr (R.A.A.) delivered the monumental Khutba (inaugural address) to the public as well as to the elite, declaring that he has been elected as their Ameer (chief) and Wali (Administrator) but in no way he is superior to them. He requested the audience to help him as long as he acted in the right direction, but may be put to right if he deviated from the right path. It was in this spirit that he managed to dispel the forces of evil by an iron hand, duly applied through his pen and sword. The letters written by the first Caliph of Islam to bring round the unruly and the turbulent element are pithy, brief, short and to the point. They are written in a very simple, factual, realistic and forceful style, avoiding bombasticism, rhetoric and superfluity. They are impressive, fact-finding, affectionate criticism of life to help maintain and establish the system of life-*Deen-e-Islam*.

Hadrat 'Umar Farooq (R.A.A.) remained the pivot of the central authority in Islam or Khalifa for about ten years from 13 A.H. to 23 A.H. During the period under reference he did not leave any thing to carry out the Commandments of the Prophet of Allah (S.A.W.) on the foot-prints left by his successor, Hadrat Abu Bakr Siddiq (R.A.A.). His tenure of service in the cause of Islam as the Khalifa in Islam was extremely engaging and busy in every moment. Not a single day passed without any engagement on the front by different commanders, provincial governors, Zakat collectors and emissaries from different parts of the Islamic State as it was the legitimate centre in Islam controlling every situation arising out from the continuous struggle to help establish and consolidate Muslim Ummah from all practical fronts of life. There was a constant flow of in-coming and out-going emissaries seeking instructions, orders and commandments regarding impending victories, diplomatic maneuvering, establishment of law and order situation, different convenants, supply of arms and ammunition, disposal of booty,

Jiziyah and *Zakat* matters including other civil and military affairs. All these state matters, more or less needed urgent, instantaneous attention of the Khalifa in Islam. In contradiction to the above cited position, there was no regular office of the Khalifa and there was a skeleton staff to look after. His mode was to write a few words on the back of the letters and applications received from concerned officials and elaborated them before those who brought them, clearly, inculcating the exact meaning and purport of the message from the central authority. In the absence of any written message from the official concerned, the instructions or orders were communicated to them on a small piece of paper or on a leather piece. The paper was pretty costly and rare during these days. During emergency and rush of work the Khalifa, 'Umar Farooq (R.A.A.) directed his secretary to write the gist of his instructions that may be conveyed to the person concerned. Thus Hadrat 'Umar Farooq (R.A.A.) disposed of so many references, queries and questions under the system mentioned above. The mode of other Khalifas regarding disposal of inquiries from far off distant places of the Islamic State was more or less the same. Whenever a commander, officer, governor, collector of Zakat or any other person received some written instructions on the back of the paper sent from the Khalifa in Islam, the same was read out to the people concerned and relevant instructions were also given by the emissaries who brought the paper. The commander-in-chief used to read out the same in front of his army, the governor before his advisers, the Zakat collector before the devotees of the *Salat* alongwith the verbal guidance on the point by the concerned plenipotentiary. Thereafter the importance of the paper lost its significance and used to be destroyed. But the same could not be wiped out from the memory of the masses and the same continued to be discussed among the forthcoming generations. Thus the importance and invulnerable value of the scribe regarding his selfless attitude, God-fearing aptitude, spirit of Jihad, legal acumen, political sagacity, welfare of the Muslims and such other sentiments should be symbolized and nurtured with the person of the scribe. Thus we find there are different versions of a particular writing attributed to the Second

Khalifa of Islam, Hadrat 'Umar Farooq (R.A.A.) on the authority of those reporting the same. There are many letters that are at variance in subject matter, variety of volume and different shades of meanings. This may be due to the reporting of the persons and the subsequent narration of the *aasaar* — reports by the persons coming after them. The writings of the Second Khalifa of Islam, Hadrat 'Umar Farooq (R.A.A.) indicate his tight, rough and tough nature as a strict disciplinarian and acute diplomat, imbibed with the spirit of truth, enforcing Shariah who would not even spare his son from the enforcement of *hudood* (divine punishment in moral turpitude). In the end, it may safely be stated that the aim and purpose of the writings attributed to the Holy Prophet Muhammad (S.A.W.) in the form of *Meesaaq-i-Madina*, the letters and despatches sent by the first lieutenant of the Messenger of Allah (S.A.W.) and the collection of instructions, guidance, orders on different petitions or despatches sent to the Second Khalifa of Islam, Hadrat 'Umar Farooq (R.A.A.) represent unanimously the one central theme — the art of managing the affairs of different ethnic groupings, based on linguistic varieties, races, castes, colours and creeds. This process continued in one form or the other whether in crude form or uniform through the Khalifa in Islam — the central authority to supervise the affairs of Muslim Ummah according to the Quraan and the practice and precept of the Sunnah of the Holy Prophet Muhammad (S.A.W.) which was abolished on 4th March 1924. Its revival is of far vital importance for the consolidation of Muslim Ummah and its regeneration among the polity of the different nations of the world. Let us arise and act !

Muhammad Adil

5

LETTERS OF HADRAT 'UMAR FAROOQ (R.A.A.)

(1)

TO ABU 'UBAIDAH BIN JARRAH (R.A.A.)

From the available historical record we find six versions of the letter addressed to Hadrat Abu Ubaidah bin Jarrah (R.A.A.) regarding his appointment as Commander-in-Chief of the forces in Syria and consequent dismissal of Hadrat Khalid bin Walid (R.A.A.). These six letters on the above cited subject vary in detail, volume and language but the subject matter is the same. Due to the high cost of paper, it was used in exceptional cases, so its use must have been restricted and could not be utilized extravagantly. Therefore the pithy, short, brief letter in substance may be considered more authentic than the more detailed, dealing with the colourful aspect of the problem. All these letters begin with the customary manner — the praise of Almighty Allah, salutations and invocation of Blessings upon the Holy Prophet Muhammad (S.A.W.) and his companions on whom peace and Blessings of Allah may shower for ever. In the usual style there is exhortation to stick to the basic principles of Justice, equity and fair play in Islamic way and practice of piety and Taqwa — the essence of *Deen* — Islamic way of life. So for the sake of brevity, we reproduce the shortest possible letter in its original translation:

In the name of Allah, All-Compassionate, Most Merciful.

Peace and Blessings of Allah from Servant of Allah Umar (R.A.A.), the commander of the believers, to Abu Ubaidah bin Jarrah (R.A.A.).

I am grateful to Allah except Whom there is none worthy of worship. Be it known to you that Hadrat Abu Bakr, (R.A.A.) the successor of the Messenger of Allah (S.A.W.) has passed away from this world.

Lo! we are all for Allah's and Lo: unto Him we are returning (2: 156)

Allah's Blessings and benedictions be upon Hadrat Abu Bakr (R.A.A.), the right in action, just to take account in legitimate affairs, soft in temperament, pious, considerate and wise. I do beseech handsome reward from Allah in this calamity, personal as well as of all Muslims. I wish to be deserving of Allah's Blessings through piety by avoiding sin and evil act. I may remain obedient to Him till death overtakes me and be graced with Paradise after death. Surely Allah has power over all things.

"I have come to know that you have beseiged Damascus. I have appointed you as the Commander-in-Chief. Muslims of Hims, and of the vicinity of Damascus as well as other Muslims, should be on consulted lest you may endanger the Muslim forces simply on account of my writing to you and the enemy be encouraged to harm you. The surplus men should be returned to me after retaining those you consider necessary, including Hadrat Khalid bin Walid (R.A.A.) without whom it may not be possible for you to carry on. (*Tahzeeb Tarikh Damishq, Ibn 'Asakir, P. 151*)

(2)

TO ABU 'UBAIDAH BIN JARRAH (R.A.A.)

The despatch under discussion deals with one of the greatest battles of Yarmuk, fiercest war fought in Syria. It is also addressed to the Commander-in-Chief of the army of the Muslim Forces-Hadrat Abu Ubaidah (R.A.A.), the custodian of the rights of Muslim Ummah, the Muhajirs and Ansars-both elite and the public in the following strains with three divergent variations, purporting to the identical theme of the despatch:

"Akhu Sumala, the messenger, had delivered your letter,

stating therein that the Byzantines have launched the attack upon the Muslims and have come with their bishops and monks to fight against you. Our Lord Almighty Allah, the only object worthy of worship, Who has blessed us and graced us always with His favours, had knowledge of it when He, the Exalted had sent down Prophet Muhammad (S.A.W.) in truth and graced him with trimph, helped him by subduing the hearts of the enemies, Whose Promise is never untrue and Who said:

> He it is Who hath sent His Messenger with the guidance and the Religion of truth, that He may cause it to prevail over all religions however much the idolators may be averse. (9:33).

So do not feel fear-stricken at the news of the numerical superiority of Byzantine army because Allah will not help them and whom God does not help, their number will not come to their rescue. Such people are left alone with their own. Do not be afraid for you are less in number because Allah is with you. You can never be less in power as Allah is with you. Remain firm wherever you are till the enemy encounters and you may gain victory through Allah's help — Who is the Best Helper and Repositor. I am surprised at your words that if the Muslims encountered the enemy they will be ruined and if they run away from the enemy, they will lose their faith (Emaan), because a formidable enemy has come to fight with them and against whom it is not possible for the Muslims to withstand and deliver the goods unless Allah may help them by sending angels or Allah may Himself come down with an army for their rescue. By God! If you did not write the last word, you would have done ill. By my life! If the Muslims remained steadfast in encountering the enemy and are slain, surely their sacrifices will not go waste. Without doubt, they will be in receipt of Divine Rewards as Almighty Allah says:

> Some of them have paid their vow by death (in battle), and some of them are still waiting, and they have not altered in the least, (33:23)

Really they are fortunate who are blessed with the honour of martyrdom. There can be a good example for the intelligent Muslims with you in those gallant fearless companions that were killed in action while fighting around the Holy Prophet Muhammad (Allah's Peace and Blessings be upon him). Those who really fight in the name of Allah, they are neither subdued nor fear death. Those who survive Prophet of Allah (S.A.W.), they were also neither afriad of death, nor of enemy, nor surrendered themselves before calamities, but always kept before them the example of their fore-runners and strived and fought to their utmost with those who opposed them or refused to accept Islam. Almighty Allah praised the persevering and the patient in the following strain:

There have been many Prophets with whom quite a number of the servants of Allah (worshippers) participated, endured hardships for the sake of Allah (the Exalted), but neither there was weakness in their conscious intention nor action, nor kneel down before the enemy but, on the contrary remained steadfast. Almighty Allah rewards the persevering in the battlefield and the following words were coming out from their mouths through their tongues.

> Our Lord! forgive our sins, ignore our short comings and irregularities, keep us steadfast before the enemy, grant us victory over the infidels. Almighty Allah, the Exalted, rewarded them with the bounties of this world and the Hereafter. Allah, the Supreme, values the virtuous. (3:147-148)

In the above noted verses, from the good of this world means the booty that falls into the hands of the victors and the good of the Hereafter means the forgiveness and grant of Paradise from Almighty Allah.

Read out this letter of mine to the people there and exhort them to give the toughest battle to the enemy to uphold the cause of Islam and endure the severest of troubles: Almighty Allah shall bless you with the bounties of this world and the Hereafter. Your statement that you have no guts to fight the enemy successfully— Surely Almighty Allah does possess this power. Our Lord, Almighty Allah, has defeated them with all their might and mean in the past. By God! If we had fought with the enemies on our own, surely we would have perished long ago. Definitely we do fight against the enemy on the basis of the trust in God, and never repose trust in our own and always pray to Allah for Help and Victory, God Willing. In any case, you will succeed, cogent need of the hour is to enkindle the real passion for sacrifices, devote to Him only under all adversity. Show patience, face the enemy with stuborn resistence, keep contingents ready, fear Almighty Allah — hope you will succeed.

'Endure outdo all others in endurance be ready, and observe your duty to Allah in order that ye may succeed.'

(3:200).

(*Futu-hush-sham, Azdi pp. 163-64*)

(3)

TO 'AMMAR BIN YAASIR (R.A.A.), GOVERNOR OF KUFA

The letter that follows relates to the appointment of the famous companion of the Messenger of Allah, Muhammad (S.A.W.), Hadrat Abdullah bin Mas'ud (R.A.A.) as *mual-lim Quraan* (Instructor in the Quraan) and Hadrat 'Ammaar bin Yaasir (R.A.A.) as governor in Kufa. More than a lac war veterans (Ghazis) were informed through the letter under reference regarding the above mentioned appointments. The letter in question is to be found in different books of history and *aa-saar*, the biographies of the companions of the Prophet of Allah (S.A.W.) in five different versions. The language may vary but the theme of the subject matter is the same. The under mentioned letter is addressed to the people of Kufa in the following strain:

I have commissioned Hadrat 'Ammaar bin Yaasir (R.A.A.) as, governor and Hadrat 'Abdullah bin Mas'ud (R.A.A.) as Instructor in the Quran and Adviser Minister and have sent them to you. Both of them are the chosen companions of the Messenger of Allah (S.A.W.), listen to them and obey them. In sending 'Abdullah (R.A.A.) to you, I have acted in a manner that entails great sacrifice on my part."

(*Ibn-Sa'd, 3/6, Tazkira-tal Huffaaz, Zehbi 1/14; Izaala-tul-*

Khifa, Wali-ullah 2/185, Kitabul-buldaan, Ibn Faqih, p. 164)

(4)

TO GOVERNOR OF EGYPT

The subject matter of the despatch relates to the fact that great famine had stricken Madina and its suburbs. So Hadrat 'Umar Farooq (R.A.A.) wrote to the Governor in Egypt, Hadrat 'Amr bin Aas, (R.A.A.) to send staple food in corn to help the afflicted area. The narrators have given five versions of the letter under reference but the sum and substance of all the five is the same — that is help in the form of food and corn for the affected people.

"Peace and Blessings of Allah, the Glorious and Exalted from the servant of Allah, 'Umar (R.A.A.) the commander of the Faithful to 'Amr bin 'Aas (R.A.A.).

By my life you and your companions enjoy full stomach and I along with my companions die due to hunger. You pay no heed! Help, Please!

(*Conquest of Egypt, by Ibn Abdul Hakam pp. 162, 163*).

(5)

TO GOVERNOR OF EGYPT

The despatch under discussion points to the cheap and short cut water way to be opened during the Caliphate of Hazrat 'Umar Farooq (R.A.A.) at the instance of Hazrat 'Amr bin 'Aas (R.A.A.). The idea was to provide facility for the people of Madina including Hijaz, easy flow of merchandize including corn etc. The water-way pointed out was the same canal dug during the days of Pharoas right from the hinder portion of River Nile to Red Sea, carry corn and merchandize in boats through the NILE to the port JAAR in Hijaz, reducing the distance to one day and night only from Madina. Prior to Islamic possession of Egypt, the canal was filled with sand due to negligence in the past. Hadrat 'Amr bin 'Aas consulted the informed circles of the Egyptians who opposed the proposal of renovating the project and the undue fear entailed that the Egyptian corn and other merchandize would be transported to Madina and Hijaz on easy and cheap terms. 'Amr bin 'Aas (R.A.A.) put up the excuse of enormous expenses involved in the undertaking, so Hadrat 'Umar Farooq (R.A.A.) became infuriated and wrote the letter in the following strain whose three different versions are available. Their sum and substance is identical that the canal should be reopened at every cost:

"Arrange to dig the canal from River NILE upto the Sea if you have to spend the entire treasury of Egypt in the undertaking." (*Ibn Abdul Hakam, p. 165*)

(6)

TO A DISTRICT OFFICER IN FARIS

The main theme of the letter under reference deals with the execution of the magicians. It is a letter addressed to the collector of a district in Faris. There are three versions of the letter, with a little variation in their contents and meanings, the three shades of the versions of the letter are available in different books of history, biographies of the companions of the Messenger of Allah, Muhammad (S.A.W.). We reproduce followwing version of the letter for the sake of brevity.

"Every sorcer or sorceress is liable to execution."

(*Tabaqat, Ibn Sa'd, 7/94*).

(7)

TO ZIMMI IMMIGRANTS OF NAJRAN

The Messenger of Allah (S.A.W.) had accorded protection of life and property to the Christians in Najran.

Before his departure from this mundane world, the Prophet and Messenger of Allah (S.A.W.) ordered that there should be no religion except Islam in Arabian peninsula: Hadrat Abu Bakr (R.A.A.) could not take action against the Christians of Najran as he was busy in quelling the rebellions throughout the length and breadth of the country. Hadrat 'Umar Farooq (R.A.A.) externed the Christians of Najran at the first opportunity. The following document was written by the Second Caliph of Islam, Hadrat 'Umar Farooq (R.A.A.) in this regard:

"This is a written document from 'Umar (R.A.A.), the Commander of the Faithful to the exiled Christians of Najran that they are under the protection of Allah, the Most High and the Exalted.

No Muslim will do any harm to them under the covenant of the Messenger of Allah (S.A.W.) and Hadrat Abu Bakr Siddiq (R.A.A.). The Governors in Iraq and Syria are directed to grant them land as soon as they reach within their jurisdiction. Whatever land they cultivate will be theirs as gift in lieu of their abondoned lands in Najran. No one will be entitled to recover the land from them so obtained. Let it be made clear that whosoever Muslim may be on the spot he should help them as they are under the protection of Islam. No Jizya will be levied upon them for twenty four months from the date of their rehabilitation in the new lands. Only revenue of the cultivated land will be realized from them without the least injustice or excess committed.

(*Ibn Sa'd 1/358; Kitabul Kharaj, Abu Yusuf, p. 73*).

(8)

TO 'AMR BIN 'AAS (R.A.A.) GOVERNOR OF EGYPT

This despatch deals with the assets and property of Hadrat 'Amr bin Aas (R.A.A.), governor of Egypt, about whom the Caliph 'Umar Farooq (R.A.A.) received the information that he is becoming richer and richer day by day at the expense of state treasury. WE are in possession of three different version of this important letter written by the

Caliph of Islam. It is forceful, expressing strong sentiments of the Caliph (R.A.A.) in anger:

"I do not want to hear the nonsensical pleadings of your case. It is useless to prive your henesty and integrity as I am sending Muhammad bin Muslima for the purpose that you hand over half of your assets to him. You are on the mainsprings of riches and offer lame excuses when caught and accounted for. You are amassing wealth for your heirs, levelling the foundations of prosperity through the help of your office. No doubt you are gathering the paraphernellia of condemnation, surely to be morsel of the Hell Fire. And Salam."

(Al-'Iqdul-Farid, Ibn Abi-al-Hadid 3/104).

LETTERS DEALING IN DEFECTIVE SUBJECT MATTER

Here we give an account of a few letters stated to be written by the second caliph of Islam, Hadrat 'Umar Farooq (R.A.A.). The Governor in Kufa was instructed by the Caliph on the subject matter regarding killing of a zimmi (a non-Muslim person under protection of Islamic state).

(9)

"Entrust the assasin Muslim to the heirs of the assassinated zimmi; they may kill him or fogive him."
(*Jaami Masaanid, Abi Hanifa Khawarzimi, Vol. 1, p. 177*).

(10)

The topic relates to the distribution of booty that fell into the hands of the victors those actually participating in the war, and those came after the end of ostility but joined the victors within three days after actual victory or till the dead bodies were buried or decomposed These are the various states of the actual problem: All these conditions have been mentioned differently in different letters, depending upon the circumstances of the case. Here we quote the most pithy, shortest possible injunction in the shape of a letter, stated to be written or ordered to be written by the Caliph to Hadrat Sa'd bin Abi Waqqas (R.A.A.) Supreme Commander of Forces in Iraq. The point at issue was the share in the booty of the conquest of Qadsiyah for the contingent of succour that reached Qudsiyah the next day after victory, headed by Qais Makshooh — who demanded his share in the booty. The matter was referred to the Khalifa for necessary elucidation. The following apt reply was received but subsequently various versions are stated to have been introduced:

"Verily booty belongs to the actual participants in the warfare."

(*Ibn-Sa'd, 3/255; Buladuri, Ansaab 1/161, Baihaqi, 6/255*).

(11)

The Khalifa, Hadrat 'Umar Farooq (R.A.A.) wrote the following to the commander of the forces during the battle of Yarmouk:

"I am pleased to know that Almighty Allah has granted victory to the Muslims through His assistance and help. The enemies are defeated. On receipt of the letter, booty may be distributed among the Muslims, special consideration should be given to those who rendered meritorious services during the battle. (*Futu-hush-Sham,1/138*).

(12)

TO GOVERNOR REGARDING IMPOSITION OF TAX ON 'AMBER'

"Amber is one of God given gifts; so realise one fifth as tax whatever is taken out from the sea including amber."

(*Ibn Salaam, p. 348*).

(13)

TO A GOVERNOR REGARDING LEVY OF TAX ON MERCHANDIZE

"When the belligerent traders enter our boundaries, realize ten percent on the merchandise as it is levied in the countries who are on war footing with the Muslims. Five percent should be exacted from the Zimmis and Muslims should be made to pay two and a half percent when the commercial merchardise is of the valuation of two hundred Dirhams and one dirham on every forty dirhams merchandize."

(*Abu Yusuf, Kitabul-Kharaj p. 78*)

LETTER TO A POLICE OFFICER IN FUSTAT

In Egypt, a Police Officer constructed a room over the roof of his house in Fustat, the Muslim neighbours complained to the Caliph, 'Umar Farooq (R.A.A.) that the Police Officer including his relations peep into the houses of their neighbours through the window or the ventilator, who wrote the following:

(14)

"I have known that Hadrat Haarija bin Huzafa has built a room over the roof of his house to peep into the neighbours' houses which should be dismantled on receipt of my letter." (*Ibn Abdul Hakam p. 104*)

(15)

The writing under reference deals with the appointments of non-Muslim mathematicians. The letter stated to have been written by the second Caliph 'Umar Farooq (R.A.A.) purports the following :

"It is an order to the governor that the non-Muslims should not be entrusted with the post or rank that has been taken away from them by AlmightyAllah. They should be kept on the footing brought down by the Omnipotant God:

and learn mathematics by yourselves.

(*Tajaarib-Umam, Ibn-e-Muskavaya 1/238*).

In fact by applying our sense of pick and choose the above cited small, pithy letters have been selected that seem to be the probable writing of the second Caliph in Islam, Hadrat 'Umar Farooq (R.A.A.) and seem to have been written by the scribe in his command by going through the huge historical record available in the form of letters pertaining to the period of the second Caliph in Islam, 'Umar Farooq (R.A.A.): The following conclusions can be aptly drawn that are equally applicable to the writings during the days of the other three rightly guided Caliphs of Islam:

(1) It is difficult to establish cent per cent verbatim veracity in the words and meanings of the letters as there was dearth of paper and proper copy of the letters was not kept due to rush of work.

(2) Letters having identical nature are apt to be close in affinity with the original letter that truly represents the personality, policy and administration of the scribe of the Caliph.

(3) In case of contradictory statements those are probably nearer to the original that are in conformity with the contents and meanings of the decisions, fatwas and conformity with the contents and meanings of the decisions, fatwas and ijtihad (re-interpretations) of the Messenger of Allah, Muhammad (S.A.W.), his respected companions or represent the personality, temperament and mode of government or the scribe of the Caliphs of Islam.

(4) The longer the letters are in volume, they are far from truth and full of additions and exaggerations.

(5) It can safely be asserted about the different letters of various versions that the common matter may represent the sum and substance or purport of the original letter. The unrelated matter represent the ingenuity of the reporters. They may have different purposes to perform. Sometime they are made to accord to the national views of the reigning Caliph, sometimes they are means to

indicate the state of God-fearing virtue of the Caliph, his piety or grandeur, personality, religious, trustworthiness, humility, justice, or his asceticism.

TO SYRIAN FRONT AND JAZIRA

The conquest of Syria and Iraq is a unique phenomenon in the history of the Muslims. In 13 A.H. Hadrat Umar Farooq (R.A.A.) became the Caliph of Islam and Muslim forces in Syria and Iraq were fighting. The forces under Khalid bin Walid (R.A.A.) and Hadrat Musanna bin Haritha (R.A.A.) had taken complete control of all the military check posts on the borders of Iraq: Consequently all the important towns and cities underlying on the right and left banks of the Eupherates up to 'Ainul Tamar and sea port Ubulla became Muslim possessions. Hadrat Khalid bin Walid (R.A.A.) addressed all the important chieftains of Iraq either to accept Islam or pay *Jiziya* or be ready to fight to settle the issue. Earlier Hadrat Abu Bakr Siddiq (R.A.A.) had despatched three armies to Syria under Amir Muawiyah's elder brother Hadrat Yazid ibn-e-Abi Sufyan, Shuraih-beel bin Hasanah (R.A.A.) and Hadrat Abu Ubaidah bin Jarrah (R.A.A.). They were under instruction to help each other and acknowledge Hadrat Abu Ubaidah bin Jarrah (R.A.A.) as their head in a battle he is actually participating. Infact the second Caliph of the Messenger of Allah, Prophet Muhammad (S.A.W.) was very keen to see the successful completion of the Syrian campaign and sent the re-inforcement (the fourth instalment) under "Amr bin 'Aas (R.A.A.) to help the centrally encamped army of the Muslims at Jabia under Abu 'Ubaidah bin Jarrah (R.A.A.).

According to one school of Muslim historians headed by Saif bin 'Umar, the Muslim forces under their respective Commanders were encamped in a vast plain near the River Yarmouk in 13 A.H. and the battle of Yarmouk was in its decisive final stage that the sad news of demise of the first Caliph in Islam reached Abu

Ubaidah bin Jarrah (R.A.A.), the supreme Commander of the Syrian expedition, who kept the news in secret alongwith the orders of the dismissal of Khalid bin Walid (R.A.A.) by 'Umar Farooq (R.A.A.) the new Caliph to himself, lest there may be any untoward happening in the Muslim forces. Earlier Hadrat 'Umar Farooq (R.A.A.) had disagreed with the then Caliph, Hadrat Abu Bakr Siddiq (R.A.A.) when the latter had declared his intention to appoint Khalid bin Walid (R.A.A.) as the supreme in command of the Muslim forces for the Syrian Expedition. But inspite of this, Hadrat Abu Bakr (R.A.A.) declined and appointed him so on his own while 'Umar Farooq (R.A.A.) had his own arguments in the following charges of complaints against Khalid bin Walid (R.A.A.):

(1) Executed the famous Arab Chieftain, Malik bin Nuwaidah whose integrity in Islam was doubtful in the eyes of Khalid bin Walid (R.A.A.) and married his wife after his assassination;
(2) While the trusted Muslims were witness to the fact that the above named chieftain was a Muslim.
(3) That the sword of Khalid (R.A.A.) is very quick in dealing with the enemies of Islam. He is more prone to fighting them to seek for peace.
(4) That Khalid bin Walid (R.A.A.) is very extravagant in squandering the Muslim public treasury through his unwarranted generosity shown to his admirers and lastly.
(5) That the great commander of the Muslim forces, Khalid bin Walid (R.A.A.) — did not maintain proper accounting of the public treasury of the Muslims and the booty that fell into the hands of the Muslim victors.

Finally 'Umar the Great (R.A.A.) was also of the view that Khalid bin Walid (R.A.A.) was almost a neo-Muslim in comparison to the old, seasoned war veterans like Abu Ubaidah bin Jarrah (R.A.A.). Therefore they are entitled to this preference according to the view point of the second Caliph in Islam. Of the Syrian conquest the battles of Yarmouk and Ajnadain were the severest. There is a variety of opinion among the historians regarding the actual dates of battle and the dismissal of Khalid bin Walid (R.A.A.) by the second Caliph in Islam, Hadrat 'Umar Farooq (R.A.A.). Regarding the dismissal of Khalid bin Walid (R.A.A.) the six versions of the despatch given in different books of histories, the following seems to be more authentic and reliable after ascertaining their contents and meanings in their historical perspectivism.

(16)

"I do hereby exhort you to fear God, the Eternal and everything is ephemeral save Him: Who has shown us the straightway from the deluded one and made us stand in light after taking us out from darkness. I have appointed you the Supreme in command of the forces of Khalid bin Walid (R.A.A.) Lookafter the Muslims as their commander-in-chief and perform the duties that are enjoined upon you in that capacity. Do not send them in perilous places in the hope of booty; before encamping make thorough acquaintance of the place and itinerary through circumspection. wherever an army is sent, take care that there should be a good numbr of *Ghazis* i.e. who fought successfully in the battle against the non-Muslims. Nothing should be done to endanger the lives of the Muslims by your actions or military expedition. Almighty Allah has put both of us under test by placing you as my dependent and myself as your officer. I do hereby enjoin upon you to safeguard your eyes from worldly riches and love of mundane wealth. Beware ! Lest the passion of the worldly belongings may not ruin you as the nations in the days gone by have been destroyed. You have seen their destruction with your own eyes (send the Muslims for the conquest of Syria). (*Tabari, vol. 4, P. 54 except the last sentence in brackets*).

(17)

TO THE MUSLIMS IN SYRIA

In elucidation of the above letter, according to Ibn A'sim Kufi, the historian, the following despatch was also sent to the Muslims in Syria:

In the name of Allah, Most Compassionate and Merciful. Merciful. Peace and Blessing of the Commander of the faithful, 'Umar bin Khattab (R.A.A.) be upon the Muslims in Syria. Be it clearly known to you that the Ummah of the Messenger of Allah, Muhammad (S.A.W.) has been deeply afflicted on account of the sad demise of Hadrat Abu Bakr Siddiq (R.A.A). Hadrat Abu Bakr Siddiq (R.A.A.) was a lover of the truth, justice and humility: he was of merciful disposition, straight forward in ordering the good and prohibiting the evil. The Ummah of the Messenger of Allah (S.A.W.) has been deprived of such a leadership: a serious lacuna has been created in the affairs of the Caliphate due to his death. But it was so ordained by Almighty Allah, everyone has to die, a human cannot do otherwise but to obey Him.

In His Hands is the last judgement and all of us shall be returned to Him ultimately. Before the occurrence of this terrible accident (death), he appointed me as his successor before the distinguished Muhajirs and Ansars (R.A.A.) and it is an extremely onerous responsibility entrusted to me. I did try to shun this responsibility but was not successful in doing so, willy nilly I had to accept it. Now it is imperative on my part to do all in my power for the welfare of the Muslims and then priorities in the matter of their organization and military expeditions. Expediency demands that Khalid bin Walid (R.A.A.) may be removed from the post of the Supreme Command of the Syrian forces and be entrusted to Hadrat Abu Ubaidah bin Jarrah (R.A.A.) Abu Ubaidah bin Jarrah (R.A.A.) will be your Supreme Commander from the time the contents of this letter are known to you. Consult him in all your affairs and act according to his advice and assessment in warfare against the enemy."

(*Ibn A'sim, P. 147*)

(18)

TO HADRAT ABU UBAIDAH BIN JARRAH (R.A.A.)

According to Futu-hush-sham, the messenger of Hadrat 'Umar Farooq (R.A.A.) reached Hazrat Abu Ubaidah bin Jarrah (R.A.A.) at a time when Khalid bin Walid (R.A.A.) had been out alongwith two Byzantine Commanders to pursue the enemy in the person of Tooma and Herbees. So Hadrat Abu Ubaidah (R.A.A.) kept the news of his appointment and demise of Hadrat Abu Bakr (R.A.A.) as secret. After a few days Khalid bin Walid (R.A.A.) returned with a large booty in the shape of the wealth of Tooma and Herbees but the news were not disclosed to him. So Khalid bin Walid (R.A.A.) sent a report of the wealth and conquest thus obtained in the name of Hadrat Abu Bakr (R.A.A.) as he was then unaware of th actual state of affairs. Naturally enough Hadrat 'Umar Farooq (R.A.A.) was infuriated and at the same time surprised to see the report but the messenger informed the Caliph 'Umar, the Great (R.A.A.) that Abu Ubaidah bin Jarrah (R.A.A.) has kept the news of his appointment as Supreme in Command as well as the demise of the first Caliph in Islam Abu Bakr (R.A.A.) as secret. Thereupon the second Caliph 'Umar Farooq (R.A.A.) convened a meeting of the elite in Madina and addressed that Khalid bin Walid (R.A.A.) was a great spend thrift, squandering money and wealth upon the pacts who recite penegyries in his praise, therefore it is necessary to remove him from his post and appoint Abu Ubaidah bin Jarrah (R.A.A.), who is a straight office and a great task master in financial dealings and accounting. So the following despatch was sent:

"*In the name of Allah, the Compassionate and Merciful.*

Peace and Blessings of Allah from Abdullah 'Umar the Commander of the Believers, to Hadrat Abu Ubaidah 'Amir bin Jarrah (R.A.A.). I am grateful to Almighty Allah, except Whom there is none worthy of worship and send benedictions and blessings upon His Prophet and Messenger, Muhammad (S.A.W.)! Be it clear that I have appointed you as supreme commander of the Muslims. Don't feel shy in accepting this: God is never ashamed of truthful statement. I do enjoin upon you to fear Almighty Allah, except Whom all is transitory, Who has brought you from the delusion of unbelief to the light of Iman (Belief). I have made you supreme commander of the forces under Khalid bin Walid (R.A.A.). Take the military force under your care and command and remove Khalid bin Walid (R.A.A.) from that post. Do not send Muslims in perilous expedition in the hope of booty, or to face the enemy when it is too large in numbers. Never say to the Muslim that I hope you will succeed in the battle, because victory is gained through complete confidence in God and not mere hoping and expectation. Do not endanger the lives of the Muslims by your action or military undertaking Shut you eyes from the sordid mundane world and set aside your heart from it. Do not do such acts that may entail your ruin in punishment as has been the case of the nations in the past which you have yourself seen and are well aware of their introvert disease. There is a slight screen in between your physical life and the hereafter. Your fore-runners have already marched off towards the hereafter and as if you are waiting for it. He is most conscious (conscentious) who fears God. Take care of the Muslims to the best of yoru ability. Wheat and barley that fell into your hands as a result of victory and about whom all of you disputed amongst yourselves, in fact, belongs to the Muslims and it is their right. Besides, whatever gold and silver came under your possession, should be distributed amongst yourselves after deducting one-fifth *(khums)* as state share. As regards your differences with Khalid bin Walid (R.A.A.) in the matter of war and peace your decision is effective and operative because you are supreme in command If peace has been ensued on the basis that wheat and barley will remain with the Byzantines as their belonging then it should be returned to them. And Peace and Blessings of Allah be upon you and all Muslims included. Khalid bin Walid, may Allah be pleased with him, has committed a mistake in attacking from the rear the fleeing foe in Marj Debaj and endangered the lives of the Muslims. And Peace and Blessing, of Allah be upon you. "(*Futu-hush-Sham*, *Egyptian Edition*, *Vol. 1*, *p. 453*).

(19)

TO HADRAT ABU UBAIDAH BIN JARRAH (R.A.A.)

"Be it clear that Hadrat Abu Bakr (R.A.A.) the true successor of the Messenger of Allah, Muhammad (S.A.W.) has breathed his last. May Allah's Blessings be upon him, the truthful, just, rightful in accountability, straight forward, humble, and soft hearted. We implore and pray Almighty Allah that He may protect us from every possible sin through His Grace, enlighten us to His obedience, grant us paradise: Surey He is All Powerful" (*Azdi*, *p. 86*, *87*).

(20)

TO HADRAT ABU UBAIDAH BIN JARRAH (R.A.A.) AND MUAAZ BIN JABAL (R.A.A.)

According to the version of the narrators of Azdi of Basra of second century Hijra, Hadrat 'Umar Farooq (R.A.A.) sent the above mentioned letter through his trusted freed slave Yarfa. Abu Ubaidah bin Jarrah (R.A.A.) did not disclose the news of the demise of Hadrat Abu Bakr (R.A.A.) except to Muaaz bin Jabal (R.A.A.). Verbally he came to know through Yarfa that 'Umar Farooq (R.A.A.) had succeeded the first Caliph, Abu Bakr (R.A.A.) and Yarfa was commissioned to find out the real condition and mode of conduct and behaviour of the Muslim military commanders in Syria viz Hadrat Khalid bin Walid (R.A.A.), Hadrat Yazid bin Abi Sufyan (R.A.A.), Hadrat Shuraih-beel bin Hasanah (R.A.A.) and Hazrat 'Amr bin 'Aas (R.A.A.). Hazrat Abu Ubaidah bin Jerrah (R.A.A.) spoke commendatory words of each of the commanders mentioned above turn by turn and sent a joint letter along with Muaaz bin Jabal (R.A.A.)

through Yarfa to 'Umar Farooq (R.A.A.). So the Second Caliph sent the following reply to the joint letter.

"*In the name of Allah, the Beneficent, the Merciful.*

Peace and Blessings of the Commander of the faithful, Amirul-Mumineen, Abdullah 'Umar to both Ubaidah bin Jarrah and Muaaz bin Jabal. I am grateful to Almighty Allah except Whom there is none worthy of Worship and enjoin both of you to be fearful of God. Fear of God engenders the pleasure of Almighty Allah and your good fortune is involved in a state of being fearful of Almighty Allah. Surely men of wisdom consider this a great boon for themselves. I am in receipt of your letter in which you have mentioned that before becoming Caliph I was on the alert to reform the self. How did you know that? These words give a sense of priase and panegyric element and simultaneously have stated that I have become the head of the Muslims: all the sundry, great and small, friend and foe, powerful and the weak — all sit before me and every one of them have their due share in the scale of my justice. Again, you have further stated to me that I should keep in mind that no excess should be committed at the time of dispensation of justice. No doubt, without the help of Almighty Allah, I cannot act rightly and you had asked me to be fearful of the Day of Accountability which is being brought nearer by the movement of night and day successively. This movement makes every new thing to become old, every far off distant thing to be nearer than before and thus brings for the every promised thing and thus with the help of this movement of time surely one day will be the Resurrection Day — When all secrets will be unfolded and the hidden evils will be brought to light when people will be standing before Almighty Allah as the very embodiment of obedience and shall be waiting in hope and fear the final decision of Allah. You write that there are people who are friend by appearance but in reality they act in secret with the enemies. In my opinion the time for this has not arrived so far this hypocracy will show itself nearer at the time of the Day of Resurrection when people will act in that strain due to fear of worldly loss or gain. You have sought protection from God that I may not understand the meaning of this letter which you never intended because you have written to me out of good wishes. So you have stated the truth I do believe it. Please do write to me occasionally because I cannot do without you. And Peace and Blessings be upon you." (*Azdi p. 89-90*).

(21)

TO HADRAT ABU UBAIDAH BIN JARRAH (R.A.A.)

According to narration of Saif bin 'Umar, the Commander-in-Chief of the Muslim forces, Abu Ubaidah bin Jarrah (R.A.A.), went out to chase the fleeing force of Byzantines after their defeat at the battle of Yarmouk. They were most probably, fleeing towards Damascus, but the informers reported that the Byzantines had changed their direction from Damascus to Fahl, a fortified town on the highway leading from Damascus to Palestine. According to other reporters it was ascertained that Heraclius had sent forces from Hams to reinforce Damascus. Ubaidah bin Jarrah (R.A.A.) and his advisers could not decide what to do. So the commander-in-chief of the Muslim forces wrote to the Caliph in Islam 'Umar Farooq (R.A.A.) for further instructions. So the following despatch from the Caliph reads as under:

"Begin with Damascus because it is the biggest fort in Syria and headquarter of the Byzantines, send contingents to Fahl, Homs and Palestine so that they may check the forces of the enemy to come to you and thus face them. If all the three above stated places are subdued before Damascus, well and good otherwise you wait till Damscus is conquered; thus leaving the contingents there you may proceed towards Fahl. if Almighty Allah grants you victory in Fahl, you along with Khalid bin Walid (R.A.A.) march towards Homs, leaving Shuraih-beel and 'Amr bin 'Aas (R.A.A.) for the conquest of Jordon and Palestine. Every area commander will be the Commander-in-Chief of the forces passing through his area till his jurisdiction is passed through." (*Tabari, Vol. IV, p. 56-57*).

(22)

TO ABU UBAIDAH BIN JARRAH (R.A.A.)

This is a despatch from 'Umar Farooq (R.A.A.) after the receipt of good news of the conquest of Damascus:

"Send back the successful warriors (Ghazis) who have come from Iraq (alongwith Khalid bin Walid (R.A.A.) and advise them to join as soon as possibly, with Said bin Abi Waqas (R.A.A.), the Commander-in-Chief of the forces in Iraq." (*Tabari Vol. 4, P. 58*).

(23)

TO ABU UBAIDAH BIN JARRAH (R.A.A.)

The son of Hadrat Abu Bakr Siddiq (R.A.A.), Abdur Rehman (R.A.A.) was a cloth merchant. In one of his commercial undertakings he happened to pass by through Damascus in Syria and accidently his eyes fell upon the beautiful charming Laila, daughter of Joodi, the Ghassani Chieftain. He was bewitched by the charm of the girl and composed verses in her praise of beauty which were widely circulated in Madina. 'Umar Farooq (R.A.A.) promised to give Laila to him provided she falls as booty in the hands of the Muslims. So the Caliph (R.A.A.) wrote the following to the Syrian Commander-in-Chief, Abu Ubaidah bin Jarrah (R.A.A.) through Hadrat Abdur Rahman bin Abu Bakr (R.A.A.).

"At the time Almighty Allah grants victory of Damascus at your hands, please give away the daughter of Joodi to Hadrat Abdur Rehman". (*Ibn-Hajar, Vol. 4, p. 404*)

(24)

TO HADRAT ABU UBAIDAH BIN JARRAH (R.A.A.)

After the conquest of Damascus a party of the Muslims committed the act of wine drinking.Abu Ubaidah (R.A.A.) complained to the Caliph, 'Umar Farooq (R.A.A.) and the following reply was received:

"Whoso drinks wine, the punishment of eighty lashes should be awarded to him. By my life, It is better for the Arabs to be poverty stricken. It was incumbent upon them to be fearful of the Almighty Allah, and worship Him, believe in Him and be grateful to Him. If any one, in future, happens to commit the wrong act of drinking wine, he should be punished according to the limits of the Law. (*Futu-hush-sham Egyptian edition Vol. 1, p. 16*).

(25)

TO HADRAT ABU UBAIDAH BIN JARRAH (R.A.A.)

The despatch under reference is in reply to the letter written by Abu Ubaidah bin Jarrah (R.A.A.) to inform the Caliph regarding the concentration of the Byzantine forces in Fahl, a city of Jordan province. This was done by the Chieftains of Jordan, who were further strengthened by the army sent by Heraclius. So the Caliph wrote the following:

In the name of Allah, Most Compassionate and Merciful.

Peace and Blessings of Allah from 'Umar, (R.A.A.) the Commander of the Believers to Hadrat Abu Ubaidah bin Jarrah (R.A.A.). I priase the Almighty Allah except Whom there is none worthy of worship. I am in receipt of your letter, mentionng the concentration of Byzantine forces and their message warning the Muslims to vacate and your reply thereto. You have supported your stand for the invasion on sound grounds. If you receive my letter after the victory over the enemy, it will be nothing new for you, because Almighty Allah, the Beneficient, had already awarded us with His bounties and graces many times, but if you happen to receive any discomfiture from the enemy, do not be afraid of it and never bow down before the enemy becuse ultimately you will succeed. The Syrian land belongs to Allah, Who will grant its victory to you and thus fulfil the prophesy of our Prophet and Messenger of Allah Muhammad (S.A.W.) So be patient and steadfast as Almighty God surely helps the persevering. Remember, if you pray to God heartily at the time of fighting the enemy, surely He will help you. O Lord! At every occasion whether past or present You have always helped the cause of your Deen and graced your faithful servants with dignity and success. Our Master Do grant them (the faithful Muslims) victory today. Do not leave them at their own; they cannot be successful by themselves except through your grace and blessing: surely: You are the Praise worthy Helpher, So by your Bounty and Blessing suppress the enemy. (*Azdi, pp. 111-112*).

(26)

TO HADRAT ABU UBAIDAH BIN JARRAH (R.A.A.)

At Fahl, the Muslim forces were waiting for the Byzantines to come out in the open field, but the people of Fahl, cut all the dams of the canals and streams, making the entire area muddy, occupied by the Muslims. Inspite of this and quite contrary to the expectations of the Byzantines, the Muslims remained firm as they were. They did not move an inch to retrace their steps. As the days passed by, the Byzantine force, comprising twenty five thousand nearly in number became straitened in supplies: So they prepared the local pupulation and landlords to supply them provision. As soon as Abu Ubaidah bin Jarrah (R.A.A.) came to know of the local situation, he despatched the contingents to the local area to conquer the arable land by sword. Thus the entire agricultural land captured by the Muslims became a disputed issue amongst them as one group demanded its distribution in the army and the other including the Commander-in-Chief, Abu Ubaidah bin Jarrah (R.A.A.) did not consider feasible to retain the land by the Muslim forces. On the other hand, they desired that the fertile arable land should remain with the local people, the former tenants etc, and revenue should be realized from them so that the future Muslim generations be benefited through its income. No understanding could be arrived at between the two above mentioned contending parties, so the matter was referred to the Caliph, 'Umar Farooq (R.A.A.) for a decision and the following reply was received:

In the name of Allah, the Beneficent, the Merciful.

Peace and Blessings of Allah be upon Abu Ubaidah bin Jarrah (R.A.A.) from Hadrat Abdullah, the Commander of the faithful. I am grateful to Almighty Allah except Whom there is none worthy of worship. I am in receipt of your letter stating that Allah has enhanced the prestige and dignity of the Believers in the *Deen* of Allah leading to the disgrace and discomfiture of the enemies. Thus facilitated our way by disposing of the wrong doers. I am really thankful to Almighty Allah Whose Bounties and Graces have always remained with us, Who has kept alive one group of the Muslims safe and graced the other with martyrdom. We fervently pray that they be benefitted with the pleasures and benedictions of Allah, implore Him that we may also be honoured through the sacrifices rendered by them, and further beseach Him that we may not be put to trial any more. They remained steadfast and faithful to Allah with all sincerity. and performed their duties with a very high and noble sense of responsibility. They always strived their all for the pleasure of Allah, thus seeking their own welfare through virtuous deeds. You have stated that the lands in Jordan had been captured by the force of arms and so one group among the Muslims is of the view that the original tillers of the soil may be rehabilitated Jiziyah should be levied upon them and they be allowed to till the soil, the other group contends that the lands have been captured by the strength of the Muslim arms so it should be distributed among the Muslims. I have considered this matter and arrived at the conclusion that the people of the conquered lands should be allowed to retain their arable lands as usual because the Muslims are not so proficient in agriculturing. The local people of the area can better perform this duty of farming then the strangers. If we enslave the local inhabitants who will look after our coming generations? By God! Neither a protected non-Muslim (Zimmi) shall talk to them nor they will be able to talk to them. Neither they will be benefitted by the wealth nor land of a Zimmi till those Muslims who enslave them are alive to be benefitted by them (the enslaved persons). When we and the enslaved people die, our offsprings will receive benefit from he issues of the enslaved persons and this state of affaris shall continue upto the Day of resurrection and these shall be the slaves of the Muslims till Islam dominates. In view of the above, please levy *Jaziyah* upon them, do not enslave them. None of the Muslims should commit any excess on them. Neither Muslims should harm them, nor should use their wealth in an unjustified manner. (*Azdi, pp 124-125*)

(27)

TO ABU UBAIDAH BIN JARRAH (R.A.A.)

On receipt of happy tidings of the conqeust of Fahl the Caliph, 'Umar Farooq (R.A.A.) wrote the followings:

"On receipt of the news of the conquest (of Fahl) feeling of happiness has been felt here and we offered thanks to Almighty Allah. It will be in the fitness of things if you stay on for sometime in the conquered land and allow rest and recreation for the army. Do not undertake any further expedition till Hadrat Sa'd bin Abi Waqqas (R.A.A.) disposes of the Persian army. God Willing there is no power to avoid evil and to do good except Allah, the most Exalted and the Supreme without Whose help it is not possible for any human being to execute any action to its end." (*Ibn-A'sim, p. 170*).

(28)

TO HADRAT ABU UBAIDAH BIN JARRAH (R.A.A.)

After the successful completion of the expedition of Fahl, Abu Ubaidah bin Jarrah (R.A.A.) appointed 'Amr bin 'Aas as governor of the land in the South East of the River Jordon and the Dead Sea and accompanied along with Khalid bin Walid (R.A.A.) to conquer Homs, a hilly province of northern Syria, studded with many forts and fortresses built in hilly hidden places. Khalid bin Walid (R.A.A.) was the leader of the Sappers and Miners and the entire Muslim army was under Abu Ubaidah bin Jarrah (R.A.A.). In short, the leadership of Khalid bin Walid (R.A.A.) and Abu Ubaidah bin Jarrah (R.A.A.) as Supreme in Command, all the important places in Homs along with their strategical forts and fortresses were subdued and the enemy sued for peace to pay Jiziyah. Some contingents were despatched to Halb where a strong fort was built. The Commander-in-Chief of the Muslim forces informed the Caliph to launch an attack upon Halb leading to the conquest of Antakia. It was at this stage that the following letter was received from the Caliph regarding the correct assessment of the position existing at that time.

"I have received your letter in which you have implored me to be grateful to Almighty Allah for the conquest of areas that came under our possession as Allah Almighty is the real conqueror for the forts and fortresses which we have been made to conquer through Divine assistance, the cities that have come under our jurisdiction and the Divine graces and benedictions that have come down to us. For all this I am really grafteful to Almighty Allah. You have stated that contingents have been sent to the Byzantine territory of Qaiser where his forces are stationed. In my opinion, this is not the right step. Recall the contingents which have been sent and stay on in Homs till the end of the year so that we may think over the next move. I do beseech the help of Allah the Exalted and the Supreme in all our affairs."*(Azdi, p. 129)*

(29)

TO JABALAH BIN AIHAM

Jabalah bin Aiham was the last Arab King of .the Ghassani Christian tribe on the Syrian frontier under Emperor Qaiser of Rome. The Emperor had sent an army of forty thousand to help Ghassani King. This force was encamped outside Damascus. The elite among the Muslims decided to invite Jabalah to Islam before actual fighting, who sent the deputation of the Muslims to Qaisar, hinting that he will also recite the Kalimah if Qaiser accepts Islam. After the Syrian conquest, the Byzantine Empire was topplied down, the near relations of Jabalah determined to become Muslims, and Jabalah himself wrote a letter to Caliph 'Umar Farooq (R.A.A.), stating that he wished to come to Madina to accept Islam. The Caliph wrote back the following in reply:

"You may come after accepting Islam and similar benefits and rights will accrue to you which we are having of course, with identical responsibilities as we are undergoing." (*Ibn- 'Abd Rabbah Al 'Iqdul Farid, Egypt 1940 edition, vol. 2 p. 56*).

(30)

TO HADRAT ABU UBAIDAH BIN JARRAH (R.A.A.)

According to Futu-hush-sham, Hadrat Abu Ubaidah bin Jarrah (R.A.A.) marched towards Homs after conquering Damascus and received the following letter from Hadrat 'Umar Farooq (R.A.A.) at a place called Ba'lBak:

In the name of Allah, the Compassionate and Merciful.

"There is no god but Allah and Muhammad (S.A.W.) is the Messenger of Allah.

Peace and Blessings of Allah from Hadrat Abdullah, the Commander of the Believers to the custodian of Ummah,

Hadrat Abu Ubaidah (R.A.A.). I am grateful to Almighty Allah except Whom there is none worthy of worship and send benedictions and blessings upon the Prophet Muhammad (S.A.W.). None can change the Commandment and Will of Allah. whoso is destined to be an unbeleiver, belief and faith (Eman) cannot be his fortune. You may be knowing that Jabalah bin Aiham of Ghassan came to me to Madina along with his nephews, cousins and the elite of the family, I entertained them all. They accepted Islam at my hands, consequently I was also pleased that Almighty Allah bestowed power to the Muslims and Islam through them. But whatever lay hidden in the unknown, I was not aware of it. We went from Madina to Makkah to perform Hajj. Jabalah circumambulated seven times round Ka'bah, the House of Allah. During circumambulation his girdle was opened as it came under the feet of a Fizzari Arab and consequently fell down from his shoulders. Jabalah looked at the Fizzari Arab with fearful eyes and said: Evil may befall you as you have made me naked in the House of Allah Fizzri said: By God! I have not done it knowingly. In spite of it, Jabalh gave blow of fist on his nose and broke his four front teeth in the mouth. Fizzari complained to me of it. I called for Jabalah and asked why he had given a fist blow to his Fizzari brother, broke his nose and four front teeth? Jabalah replied, "He opened my girdle by pressing it through his foot. By God! Had there been no consideration for the respect of Baitullah (House of God), surely I would have killed him." I said to him, "Now you have confessed the guilt, either he may forgive you or I shall take vengeance." Jabalah said: "vengeance shall be taken from me, although I am a king and he is an ordinary petty Arab? I said to him: Look here! Both of your are Muslims, only by your good manners, you can gain superiority over him. Jabalah demanded respite for a day: I asked Fizzari who agreed to it. In the midst of night, Jabalah along with his brothers rode back on camels to Syria and sought shelter with Kalabut-taghia (The Byzantine Qaiser). I do hope that he will fall into your hands. Wait after the conquest at Homs, do not march forward. If the people of Homs sue for peace in lieu of Jiziyah so much the better but if they do not, fight with them; send your informers to

Antakia, (the headquarter of the Byzantine Emperor) and be aware of the Syrian Christian Arabs. Peace and Blessings of Allah be upon you and upon all Muslims. (*Futu-hush-sham, Vol. 2, p: 30*).

(31)

TO ABU UBAIDAH BIN JARRAH R.A.A.)

According to Saif-bin 'Umar, Heraclius left his headquarter in Antakia and proceeded to Roha, the Capital of Mesopotamia. Hadrat Abu Ubaidah bin Jarrah (R.A.A) informed the Caliph 'Umar Farooq (R.A.A.) regarding the movement of Heraculius along with the good tidings of the conquest of Homs: in reply the Caliph sent the following despatch:

"You may stay in Homs and invite to join the fold of Islam the powerful and the brave Syrians of Arab Christain tribes. Rest assured, God Willing, I will keep in constant flow the supply of provisions." (*Tabari Vol. 4, p. 154*).

(32)

TO ABU UBAIDAH BIN JARRAH (R.A.A.)

According to the version of Futu-hush-sham, Hadrat Abu Ubaidah bin Jarrah (R.A.A.) came to Homs suddenly after subduing the northern Syria resulting in the allegiance of the governors of Jasia and Bal-bak after payment of Jiziyah. Naturally the Governor of Homs could not make any preparation and sued for peace in a temporary capacity for one year with the intention to meet the Muslims in the field next year after due preparations. A portion of the Muslims forces proceeded to Halb and Qinnisrin, the frontier portion of the Syrian territory, under the command of Khalid bin Walid (R.A.A.) and attacked the rural area. Thereupon, the governor Qinnisrin also sought peace for payment of Jiziyah at least for one year. The natural consequence of all the above victories resulted in the temporary inaction or suspension of movement of Muslim forces. For sometime there was no correspondance between the Caliph 'Umar Farooq (R.A.A.) and Abu 'Ubaidah bin Jarrah (R.A.A.), so the Caliph thought that the Muslims were suffering from inertia and therefore, were avoiding Jihad in the Cause of Allah. So the above state of affairs could not be tolerated by the Caliph 'Umar Farooq (R.A.A.) and the following despatch is the result:

In the name of Allah, Most Compassionate and Merciful.

Peace and Blessings of Allah be upon the Custodian of Ummah, Abu 'Ubaidah 'Aamir bin Jarrah (R.A.A.) from Abdullah, 'Umar bin Khattab, (R.A.A.) the Commander of the Believers. I am grateful to Allah except Whom there is none worthy of worship and send benediction upon His Porphet and Messenger, Muhammad (S.A.W.) I do beseech you to be fearful of Allah, the Supreme, the Exalted and shun the commission of sin in the limits set by Allah, the Supreme in all spheres both internal and external. I further warn you to be not akin to those about whom Allah, the Almighty has declared the following through His Messenger, Muhammad (S.A.W.):

"Say: If your fathers and your sons, and your brothers, and your wives, and your tirbes, and the wealth you have acquired and merchandize for which ye fear that there will be no sale and dwellings ye desire are dearer to you than Allah and His Messenger and striving in His way. then wait till Allah bringeth His command to pass. Allah guideth not wrong-doing folk." (9:24),

(*Futu-hush-sham, Vol. 1, p 66*)

(33)

TO ABU 'UBAIDAH BIN JARRAH (R.A.A.)

According to the version of Futu-hush-sham, the people of Halb had sued for peace with Abu 'Ubaidah bin Jarrah (R.A.A.), but the Byzantine Governor fortified himself in a strongly built fortress out side Halb as he was against this peaceful move of the people of the city. The seige of the fort continued for several months. The Byzantines raided the Muslims during night and stoned them from the fortress. The seige lasted for many months. There was no hope of its victory. The Muslims were also tired on account of this state of affairs. Hadrat Abu 'Ubaidah bin Jarrah (R.A.A.) was waiting for the conquest so that he may write to the Caliph. On the other hand, Caliph 'Umar Farooq (R.A.A.) was anxiously waiting to hear soon from the frontier, so in his anxiety the Caliph wrote the following:

"*In the name of Allah, the Beneficent, the Merciful.*

I am thankful to Almighty Allah except Whom there is none worthy of worship and send my benedictions to Prophet Muhammad (S.A.W.). I am highly anxious to know your welfare and the well-being of our Muslim brothern. It seems that this anxiety is like a cancer eating away the body. Day and night I am anxiously waiting for your messenger and am unable to understand as to why your *qasid* or letter is not coming. It appears that you wish to write only to send the good tidings of victory and state-booty. O 'Ubaidah! (R.A.A.) although I am far away from you but my heart is with you all through praying for your safety and welfare my heart is anxious to know your well-being as the anxious mother waits for the welfare of her child. After going through this letter, take such suitable steps that may strengthen Islam and thus the bands of the Muslims become strong. And Peace and Blessings of Allah be upon you."

(*Futu-hush-sham Vol.1, p. 156, Egypt*).

(34)

TO ABU UBAIDAH BIN JARRAH (R.A.A.)

The chain of narrators of Futu-hush-sham state that the outer fortress of Halb could not be subjugated although the seige lasted for more than five months so it was decided that the seige may be lifted so that the governor of Halb may be in the open field. On reaching Halb, Hadrat Abu Ubaidah bin Jarrah (R.A.A.) informed the Caliph, 'Umar Farooq (R.A.A.) regarding the conquest of Qinnsirin, part of Halb, successful raids on the cities lying on Syrian frontiers and receding their steps from the outer fortress of Halb. The following reply was received from the Caliph:

"Your messengers reached here and delivered the happy news of the conquests gained over the enemy along with the information of those who fell martyrs. You have further stated that the seige of Halb has been abandoned and the forces encamped in the area lying between Antakia and Halb. In my view, this move of yours is not proper. You have allowed a person to go scot free whose country and capital, Halb, has already been conquered by you. The news will be set afloat that you could do nothing of the man, thus resulting in the loss of your prestige and increase in the enemys' pomp and power. The subdued people will get courage to fight with you — the elite and the common man, all and sundry of the Byzantine forces. The informers of the governor will inform them about your activities and the Syrian officials of the government will correspond with each other to renew hostilities with you. So wage war against the governor till Almighty Allah kills him, or he may be given in your possession or peace or defeat may be decided. Despatch raiding contingents throughout the area of Eupherates - plains, hilly unsurmountable tracts and narrow valleys. Make peace with those who are willing to sue for peace after payment of *Jiziyah.* I entrust you including all Muslims in the peaceful custody of Allah the Supreme. I am sending along with this letter an army desiring to lay down its lives in the cause of Allah. The army is comprised of the Arabs, Muwalis, infantry and horsemen of Hadramaut and Yaman. Besides, regular succour shall continue flowing in, God Willing. Peace and Blessings of Allah be upon you. (*Futu-hush-sham Vol. 1 p. 160*).

(35)

TO HADRAT ABU UBAIDAH BIN JARRAH (R.A.A.)

The battle of Yarmouk was the last and final attempt of the Byzantine Emperor to expel the Muslims from their territory after the conquest of Homs in 15 A.H. There was an hair breath escape of Muslims from sustaining defeat. The Arab narrators have mentioned Muslims as forty three thousand while the Byzantine forces were calculated to be more than 4 Lacs — this representing a ratio of 1 to 9. The Commander-in-Chief of the Muslims wrote to the Caliph, 'Umar Farooq (R.A.A.) apprising him of the entire exact local situation in the matter, informing him that the Byzantine Emperor, Heraclius, has invited the forces from all the provinces, fully armed to undergo any ordeal against the Muslims - a spectacle of collection of forces seldom seen and performed by any previous emperor. We are to be attacked soon by the enemy. After circumspection we have decided to leave Homs for Damascus as the local population around Homs could not be trusted upon in spite of the formidable fort of Homs we occupy. Further we are deficient in men and material in comparison to the enormous physical strength of the enemy. Therefore, we pray and ask you for help. The following is the reply of the Caliph, Hadrat 'Umar Farooq (R.A.A.):

In the name of Allah, Most Compassionate and Merciful.

Peace and Blessings of Allah from Ameerul Mumineen be upon Abu 'Ubaidah bin Jarrah (R.A.A.), his companions both Muhajireen and Ansar, Companions of the Companions as well, including other Mujahideen. I am grateful to Almighty Allah except Whom there is none worthy of worship.

It has come to my notice that you have left Homs for Damascus, thus abandoning the land to the enemy that Allah had bestowed upon you. I do not approve of it. I asked your messenger whether this action has been taken by the unanimous will and approval of all who replied in the affirmative testifying to the fact that it was done, under the advice of th elite and the mature and experienced officers of the army. Subsequently I came to the conclusion that the action taken was unanimous as it received the approbation of all, therefore there must come out good out of it for the present and the hereafter This consideration subsequently subsided my disapproval and anger. Your ambassador has asked for provision. Rest assured, supplies in provision will reach you, God Willing, before the receipt of this letter. You should remember that neither (during Prophet's time) did we defeat the enemy on account of the overwhelming majority of our forces nor Almighty Allah caused victory to descend upon us through sheer majority force, on the contrary; often Almighty Allah abandoned the majority force of the enemy: consequently they were defeated and their majority did not benefit them. Often Almighty Allah bestows victory upon small force in comparison to the huge number. Let us pray to Allah that He may grant us victory over the common enemy and bring ruin and chastisement upon him: And Peace and Blessings of Allah be upon you." (*Azdi, p. 141*)

(36)

TO HADRAT ABU 'UBAIDAH BIN JARRAH (R.A.A.)

Commander-in-Chief, Hadrat Abu 'Ubaidah bin Jarrah (R.A.A.) came to know at Yarmouk, where he along with other Syrian Commanders had stationed to fight against the Byzantines, that they were several lacs in number and had come to fight and expel the Muslims from there by themselves. Several thousand religious leaders of the Byzantine Empire had joined it either to participate in the religious war against the Muslims or to stir up the religious and fighting fervour of the army. The number of the enemy far exceeded the expectations of the Muslims. Consequently they felt unnerved as they were near about Forty thousand only. After consulting the advisers, the Commander-in-Chief, wrote an urgent letter to the Caliph, 'Umar Farooq (R.A.A.), stating that the Byzantines have attacked the Muslims by land and sea, recruited every capable person to handle weapons; bishops, priests and monks have left their places of worship to join the army to uphold the cause of Roman Imperialism. The Roman Emperor had gathered armies from the provinces of Armenia and Mesopotamia as well: The total strength was calculated to be four lacs. As soon as these facts came to my knowledge I did not consider it proper to keep the Muslims in the dark from the actual position, so I consulted them and it was decided that all the Muslims should go away to isolated parts of Syria and gather their scattered army. After the receipt of military help from your quarter, we may go forth to fight the enemy. Speedy action to provide succour to the encircled army was recommended by the Commander-in-Chief to the Caliph in Islam, 'Umar Farooq (R.A.A.). Special request was made to send army after army and it was further stated that if the Muslims remained inactive lying at Yarmouk, it was quite possible they may perish and if they ran away they will lose their faith-*Deen*. Their enemy with whom they are to fight, is so powerful that they are incapable to deliver the good against him unless Allah, the Almighty may send angels for their help or He may Himself come with an army. In reply thereto Caliph 'Umar Farooq (R.A.A.) wrote the following:

"Akhu Sumala (Abdullah bin Qarat) came with your letter. You have stated that the Romans have invaded the Muslims from land and sea and brought their priests and monks to fight with you. No doubt, our Supreme Master, Whom we praise and pray, Who is our resolver of difficulties and the Greatest Benefactor, constantly confering His benedictions and Blessings upon us, knew the presence of these priests and monks when He (Almighty Allah) sent the truthful Prophet Muhammad (S.A.W.) into this world, graced His beloved Prophet with conquests, helped and encouraged him (S.A.W.) by creating awe into the hearts of the enemy. None of His Promises can be untrue. He (Allah) is Alone Who has sent His Messenger, Muhammad (S.A.W.) with a Book of Guidance, revealing the true way of life.

> Fain would they put out the light of Allah with their mouths, but Allah disdaineth (aught) save that He shall perfect His light, however much the disbelievers are averse. He is Who hath sent His Messenger with the guidance and the Religion of truth, that He may cause it to prevail over all religions, however much the idolators may be averse.(9 : 32, 33).

So you should never be afraid of the Byzantines because Allah will not help them. And whoso is not helped by Almighty Allah, the numerical strength of the army is of nc avail for him as such a person is left aside by Almighty Allah. You should also not be afraid of the less number of your army as God is with you and with whosoever God is, one is not deficient. Remain steadfast wherever you are till the encounter with the enemy and the victory with the help of God - He is the Best Protector, and Omnipresent Helper.

I am surprised by your words that "if the Muslims, remained as they are before the enemy take it, they are ruined, if they flee away from the enemy their Iman (faith) will be destroyed as it is beyond their power to overcome such a formidable foe, except that Almighty Allah may help them by sending angels or Himself come to help them with the army." By God! if you did not mention these words of exception surely you would not have done good. By my life! if the Muslims remained firm, patient and killed in action, their sacrifice will not prove in vain in the sight of Allah the Supreme, for He say:

> Of the believers are men who are true to that which they covenanted with Allah, some of them have paid

their vow by death (in battle), and some of them are still waiting and they have not altered in the least. That Allah my reward the true men for their truth. (33: 23,24).

For an intelligent person, there is an example of those who were killed in action while fighting around the Holy Prophet Muhammad (S.A.W.). Those actually fought along-with the Prophet of Allah (S.A.W.), they neither felt them-selves powerless nor were afraid of death. Those also who survived the Prophet of Allah (S.A.W), were neither afraid of death nor of the enemy nor succumbed to the impending perils or tribulation: on the contrary they put the example of their forerunners before them and fought against those who opposed them in the way of Allah or refused to accept Islam. But the believing Muslims remained steadfast and patient. Allah, the Almighty has praised them in the following words of the Quran.

> "And with how many a Prophet have there been a number of devoted men who fought (beside him). They quailed not for aught that befell them in the way of Allah, nor did they weaken, nor were they broght low. Allah loveth the steadfast. Their cry was only that they said; Our Lord! Forgive us for our sins and wasted efforts, make our foothold sure, and give us victory over the disbelieving folk. So Allah gave them the reward of the world and the good reward of the Hereafter, Allah loveth those whose deeds are good."
> (3: 146 to 148).

The above verses of the Quran are explicit in blessings of this world which are victory and booty: Forgiveness from sins and paradise in the Hereafter. Please read out this letter of mine to the people, exhort them to face the enemy bravely for the prepondarance of Islam. Be patient during extreme diversity: God will bless them with the blessings of this world and the hereafter. Your assertion that the Muslims are faced with an enemy whom they cannot overcome. If you do not possess that capability, Allah, the All-Powerful has. Our Lord Allah had been continuously defeating them. By God! if we were to fight with the enemy with our own, surely we would have been perished long ago by the enemy: We fight only in reposing our confidence in God and never put our trust in ourselves except Allah, and pray to Him for victory and blessedness. God Willing, you will succeed in the end: the only need of the hour is the real spirit for sacrifice in the way of Allah and pray to Him in each and every encounter, be patient; remain steadfast in front of the enemy keep your contingents ready and be fearful of God only. There is every hope that you will succeed.

"Endure, out do all others in endurance, be ready, and observe your duty to Allah in order that ye may succeed." (3: 200) (*Azdi- pp. 163-164*).

There is no mention in the letter cited above regarding despatch of succour of army men but in 'Futuh by Ibn-A'sim there is a specific reference of the promise by Hadrat 'Umar Farooq (R.A.A.) for provision of military aid and despatched a contingent of three thousand horsemen. According to Futu-hush-sham the armed help consisted of seven thousand riders. There are four different versions of the letter under reference with little or no variations.

(37)

TO HADRAT ABU 'UBAIDAH BIN JARRAH (R.A.A.)

During the battle of Yarmouk several critical stages presented themselves so much so that the forces of the enemy ransakced the rank and file of Muslims encamping the women and children, ultimately the Muslims were victorious. Hadrat Abu 'Ubaidah bin Jarrah (R.A.A.) sent the letter of good news to Madina and the following reply of Hadrat 'Umar Farooq (R.A.A.) was rceived by him:

"Greetings and Salutation to Abu 'Ubaidah bin Jarrah (R.A.A.) from the servant of Allah, 'Umar, the Commander of the Faithful. I am grateful to Almighty Allah except

Whom there is none worthy of worship. I am in receipt of your letter and am happy to note that All-Powerful Allah has destroyed the polytheists, bestowed victory upon the Believers, blessed the faithful and the obedient, so I am grateful to Allah, the Sacred, for all His Blessings and Graces shown upon us and beseech Almighty Allah for the completion of these Blessings and Benedictions. Be it clear that you were victorious not because of your numerical strength, power or paraphernelia of warfare but through Divine Help, Grace and Benediction. He is Alone Powerful, the Sacrosanct, Best Creator, Deserving of All-Praise and Cherisher of the entire universe:

So glorified be, Allah, the Best of Creators!" (23:14)

So Allah's praise is due to Him and Peace and Blessings be upon you. (*Azdi, p. 221*).

Ibn-A'sim has also narrated similar version of this letter with little variation as regards meaning and contents except specific direction from the Caliph, 'Umar Farooq (R.A.A.) for distribution of booty with special consideration to the deserving who had shown extra ordinary bravery and remarkable service during warfare against the enemy. Yaqubi has stated a queer version regarding the booty that fell into the hands of the victors that the same be kept intact till the conquest of Jerusalem.

(38)

TO HADRAT ABU 'UBAIDAH BIN JARRAH (R.A.A.)

According to the explanation given in Futu-hush-sham, attributed to Waqidi that Hadrat Abu 'Ubaidah (R.A.A.) distributed the booty of Yarmouk among the army. Muslims had two kinds of horses pure Arabic horses and mixed breed. Hadrat Abu 'Ubaidah bin Jarrah (R.A.A.) gave double share to the pure Arab horse owners and single share to the pure Arab horse owners and single share to the mixed breed. People objected to this discriminatory treatment. The Commander-in-Chief replied that he had before him the example of the Prophet of Allah, Muhammad (S.A.W.) Even thereupon people were not satisfied. So Hadrat Abu 'Ubaidah (R.A.A.) had to refer the matter to 'Umar Farooq (R.A.A.), the Caliph and the following reply was received:

"You have acted exactly in accordance with the command and practice of the Prophet of Allah (S.A.W.). The Arab horse should get double share while the mixed one should receive single - the discrimination allowed by the Messenger of Allah (S.A.W.) after the battle of Khaiber.
(*Futu-hush-sham - Egypt Vol. 1, p. 138*).

(39)

TO HADRAT ABU 'UBAIDAH BIN JARRAH (R.A.A.)

After the battle of Yarmouk, Hadrat Abu 'Ubaidah (R.A.A.) and Hadrat Khalid bin Walid (R.A.A.) chased the defeated Romans upto Homs - the northern province of Syria. The Governor of Homs declared that they abide by the covenant, therefore, they were not to be touched. There were several forts and cities of vital importance in the territory of Homs. They were to be conquered. In the first instance the people of Qinsirin, important big citadel in the north, were made to pay Jiziya. Thereafter Halb, the famous and strong fortress was beseiged whose governor acceeded to pay Jiziya. After its capture, Hadrat Abu 'Ubaidah conquered Antakia - the last city of Syria, situated in the lap of the mountain and connected with the Mediterranian Sea through a port about six miles in the south. The road passing through Antakia was the one coming from Constantinople to Syria. Keeping in view of its importance the Caliph wrote the following to Abu Ubaidah bin Jarrah:

"Maintain a contingent army of the Muslims, saturated with spirit of Jehad and goodness. The contingent Muslim army should remain posted firmly. Pay them salary regularly."
(*Buladuri, p. 153*).

(40)

ADDRESSED TO ABU 'UBAIDAH BIN JARRAH (R.A.A.)

In the name of Allah, All Compassionate and Most Merciful.

From the servant of Allah, 'Umar bin Khattab (R.A.A.) to the Governor of Syria, Abu 'Ubaidah bin Jarrah (R.A.A.).

I am grateful to Almighty Allah except Whom there is none worthy of worship and send blessings upon His Prophet (S.A.W.). Your letter has been delivered here wherein you have asked about the area upon which you should concentrate after the battle of Yarmouk. In this matter, the advice of the nephew of the Prophet and Messenger of Allah (S.A.W.) Hadrat Ali (R.A.A.) is that Jerusalem should be beseiged. Almighty Allah will surely make this city subdued at your hands. Peace and Blessings of Allah be upon you." (*Futu-*
(*Futu-hush-sham*, *Egypt*, *Vol. 1*, *p. 139*).

(41)

THE TREATY OF ELIA (JERUSALEM)

The most sacred city of the Jews and the Christians was beseiged several times but the elite of the place did not surrender because of the promise of help from Kaiser. After the conquest of Yarmouk and consequent capture of the abandoned territory by the Syrian Government, Hadrat Abu 'Ubaidah bin Jarrah (R.A.A.) renewed the seige of ELIA and straitened it then before the inhabitants of the city lost hope of the expected contingent and became ready to accept the payment of Jiziyah on condition that the Caliph. 'Umar Farooq (R.A.A.) should come in person and authenticate the treaty regarding payment of Jiziyah under his own signature. Hadrat Abu 'Ubaidah bin Jarrah (R.A.A.) accepted the stipulation, sent for the Caliph 'Umar

Farooq (R.A.A.) who came to Elia and gave the following in writing.

"In the name of Allah, All Compassionate and Most Merciful.

The inhabitants of ELIA are granted protection of their lives, property, synogogues, cross, the sick and the healthy of the Place including every religion and nation by the servant of Allah, 'Umar (The Caliph R.A.A.). The places or worship will neither be used for residential purposes nor destroyed nor their attached properties shall be confiscated. Neither their cross of gold and silver, pelf and wealth shall be reduced nor will they be forced to change their religion, nor will be harmed in any possible manner, nor any Jew shall live and remain with them. It is incumbent upon the people of Elia to pay as much Jiziyah as the inhabitants of other cities of Syria, to turn out the Byzantines and the dacoits. The Byzantine people leaving Elia shall enjoy protection of life and property till they enter the territory of Byzantine government. Those who desire to stay on, are allowed to do so provided they pay Jiziyah equal to the amount paid by the other inhabitants of Elia. Further, among the people of Elia, deserving to accompany the Byzantines along with their wealth and leaving their chruches, crosses will remain safe till they enter the area of Byzantine government. Before the arrival of this humbleself, the peasant present, may remain in Elia by paying Jiziyah equal to the amount paid by other persons. Those desirous to go with the Byzantines are allowed to do so. Those who want to return to their respective rural areas along with their family and children are also allowed to do so and the revenue shall not be charged from them till the next harvest time. Whatever has been covenanted in the document is hereby witnessed by Almighty Allah and His Messenger, Muhammad (S.A.W.), his lieutnants and Muslims on condition that the people of Elia remain regular in the payment of Jiziyah.

(*Tabari, Vol. 4. p. 159*).

There is another version of treaty with little or no variation in substance.

(42)

TO THE PROVINCIAL GOVERNORS

One day Hadrat 'Umar Farooq (R.A.A.) was entertaining the Muslim Ghazis after the treaty of Elia, a renowned monk came to the Caliph, 'Umar (R.A.A.), presented a preparation of Syrup and siad: This syrup is very useful for health. Kindly do take it. The Caliph asked regarding the ingredients of the Syrup; so the monk explained that is prepared by the juice of grapes by putting it on fire it is reduced to one-third and used as Syrup. Hadrat 'Umar Farooq (R.A.A.) put his finger into it and said that is is hard like coaltar; when he drank it it was found to be tasty. The Caliph instructed the Syrian commanders of the army that they should arrange this drink for the army and also wrote the following letter to other provincial governors:

"I was given a Syrup prepared by the juice of grapes by putting the same on fire till the same is reduced to one third and is akin to coaltar. The Muslim fighters in the way of Allah should be provided this Syrp as Government ration." (*Tabari*, *Vol. 4*, *p. 161*).

There are a few historians who ascribe the above cited letter to be written in the name of 'Ammaar bin Yasir (R.A.A.). This, they state was written to him by the Caliph, 'Umar Farooq (R.A.A.) after the conquest of Elia in 16 or 17 A.H. According to them the following version seems to be more appropriate:

"I went to Syria. The people of the place brought a Syrup whose ingredients was the juice of the grapes which is put on fire till it is reduced to one third. Thus it becomes lawful or as its forbidden portion is burnt away. The Muslim fighters in the cause of Allah under your command should be ordered to take this Syrup. Peace and Blessings of Allah be upon you." (*Azdi*, *p. 231*).

(43)

TO HADRAT ABU 'UBAIDAH BIN JARRAH (R.A.A.)

The letter cited below was written by Hadrat 'Umar Farooq (R.A.A.) to Hadrat Abu 'Ubaidah bin Jarrah (R.A.A.) It was received by the addressee at the place known as Jaabiyah.

"Peace and Blessings from the servant of Allah, 'Umar (R.A.A.), the commander of the Believers to Abu 'Ubaidah bin Jarrah (R.A.A.).

Let it be known that Government of Islam can only be established by a person possessing maturity in planning, always alert in the execution of its duties, enjoys spotless conduct in the estimation of the public, does not possess a single iota of ill-will in his heart against the people, never cares for any insult while executing the right action or uttering the truth." (*Buladuri*, *Al-Ansaab Vol. 9*, *p. 595*).

(44)

TO HADRAT ABU 'UBAIDAH BIN JARRAH (R.A.A.)

A Muslim murdered a zimmi (person under the protection of the Muslim state). Abu 'Ubaidah (R.A.A.) could not decide the nature of punishment to be awarded to the wrong doer Muslim. So the matter was referred to the Caliph, 'Umar Farooq (R.A.A.) for decision. The following reply was received:

"If the Muslim is an habitual murderer, his neck should be chopped off from his body or if he has killed the *zimmi* due to extreme rage and sudden furiousness, four thousand *dirhams* should be taken from him as blood money and distributed among the lawful heirs of the deceased.

(*Kanzul Ummall, Baihaqi, Vol. 7, p. 303*).

(45)

TO HADRAT ABU 'UBAIDAH BIN JARRAH (R.A.A.)

During the practice of arrow-marking in Syria, an arrow from a Muslim pierced into the body of a small child sitting into the lap of his maternal uncle and the infant died instantaneously. There was no other close relation of the deceased. Hadrat Abu 'Ubaidah (R.A.A.) referred the matter to the Caliph, 'Umar Farooq (R.A.A.) regarding distribution of the blood money. The following was received in reply thereto:

"The Messenger of Allah (S.A.W.) used to say that any one not possessing a caretaker to look after him, his master and care taker is Allah and His Messenger (S.A.W.) So if a person does not have any lawful heir, his maternal uncle can be so." (*Baihaqi, Vol. 6, p. 214*).

(46)

TO HADRAT ABU 'UBAIDAH BIN JARRAH (R.A.A.)

I have known that Muslim women take bath along with Zimmi (Protected by the state who is not Muslim) women. They should be forbidden to do so."

(*Kanzul 'Ummaal Vol 8, p. 214*).

According to another narration there was an addition of the words "that it is not proper for a Muslim woman who believes in Allah and the Final Day of Judgement to show her body to a non-Muslim woman."

(47)

TO HADRAT ABU 'UBAIDAH BIN JARRAH (R.A.A.)

I am writing this letter to you because in doing so I have done my best for the mutual welfare of both of us. Adhere to the five fundamental principles so that your

'Deen' will be safe and you will attain utmost felicity and good fortune. When two persons present their case before you, you should ask the plaintiff to produce true and just witnesses and ask the defendant to take on firm and solemn oath. Treat the poor with sympathy, encourage him to open his mouth i.e. to speak out frankly what is in his mind. Be considerate towards the alien because if he has to stay on for long, he will quit his due right, return to his native place and thus you will be responsible for the relinquishment of his just right as you did not show sufficient regard for him. Be extremely judicious towards both - the plaintiff and the defendant, try your utmost to make a compromise between the two contending parties till you reach the correct decision. (*Kitabul Kharaj - Abu Yusuf, p. 117*).

The above despatch has been reported by different historians and scholars of repute with a few variations. Some of them have ascribed the same to other persons like Hadrat Abu Musa Ashari and Hadrat Amir Muawiya (R.A.A.).

(48)

TO HADRAT ABU 'UBAIDAH BIN JARRAH (R.A.A.)

The property belonging to the Muslims but in possession of non-Muslims happens to become the possession of the Muslims as booty, that portion of such assets should be returned before distribution to the Muslims actually belonging to them and are in a position to recognize the same as their own. (*Mudaw-wana-tul-Kubra, Vol. 1, p. 376*).

(49)

The Syrian Ghazis (actual fighters in the way of Allah) requested Hadrat Abu 'Ubaidah (R.A.A.) to take Zakaat belonging to their horses and slaves, who declared that horses and slaves are exempt from payment of *Zakaat.* The Ghazis referred the matter to the Caliph, 'Umar Farooq (R.A.A.) who also refused to accept

Zakaat on horses and slaves. These Ghazis again pressed Hadrat Abu 'Ubaidah bin Jarrah (R.A.A) and insisted on him to accept Zakaat against their horses and slaves. The matter was finally referred to the Caliph in Islam, 'Umar Farooq (R.A.A.) by Abu 'Ubaidah bin Jarrah (R.A.A.) and the following order was received:

"If these people like that Zakaat may be realized from them, return the same to them and the ration for their slaves may be fixed by you on behalf of government."

(*Muwatta p. 121*).

(50)

TO KHALID BIN WALID (R.A.A.)

Khalid bin Walid (R.A.A.) took bath in one of the Syrian Public Bathrooms. The body was massaged by a mixture called 'Usfur, prepared through meading with wine. The incident came to the notice of the Caliph in Islam, Hadrat 'Umar Farooq (R.A.A.), who despatched the following:

"It has been brought to my notice that you have got your body massaged with wine, although wine (*Khumr*) has been declared by Almighty Allah as one of the prohibitions, whether it may be pure or mixed with something else: as commission of introvert and extrovert sins are prohibited just as Almighty God has forbidden drinking of wine, so it is not permissible to touch it, save that t is necessary to remove it through washing and cleansing. Be it clear that wine is pure filth, its touching is not allowed, if it is done through mistake, the same should not be repeated again."

(*Tabari Vol. 4*, *p. 204*).

(51)

The above cited letter has been reported with a few variations, using stronger language for Khalid bin Walid (R.A.A.) that he was born to be burnt in hell-fire etc.

Khalid bin Walid (R.A.A.) wrote in explanation that ubtan (Powder) was prepared in a mixture of water and wine that wine had come under the category of water. Hadrat 'Umar Farooq (R.A.A.) got annoyed and wrote:

"I am of the view that the off-shoots of Mughira (Khalid bin Walid (R.A.A.) have became obstinate. May Almighty Allah not cause you to die in this state."

(*Tabari, Vol. 4, p. 204*).

(52)

TO HADRAT ABU 'UBAIDAH BIN JARRAH (R.A.A.)

In 17 A.H. the headquarter of Qaiser, Antakia, the most beautiful city of northern Syria was conquered by the Muslims. The Governor of Syria, Abu 'Ubaidah bin Jarrah (R.A.A.), sent the good news of its conquest to 'Umar Farooq (R.A.A.), the Caliph and also stated that the place is so beautiful, fascinating and alluring that apprehension came to my mind that if the Arabs are allowed to continue to stay on there, it is quite possible that they may become addicted to pleasure seeking activities, so I returned soon to Halb. The Governor further sought instructions regarding advancement of army and to continue military advance against the Byzantine or to wait for some time. The Governor also complained that the Arabs are being infatuated by Byzantine women and are desirous to marry with them. Hadrat 'Umar Farooq (R.A.A.) replied the following:

"*In the name of Allah, the Compassionate and the Merciful.*

Peace and Blessings of Allah from His servant, 'Umar to the Governor of Syria, Abu 'Ubaidah bin Jarrah (R.A.A.). I am grateful to Almighty Allah except Whom there is none worthy of worship and send my blessings and salutations upon the Prophet and Messenger of Allah, Muhammad (S.A.W.) I am further thankful to Almighty Allah for the conquest bestowed upon the Muslims, Who has promised special Blessings and Graces for the virtuous in the Hereafter and Who has been kind to us always and helping us throughout. You have stated, that Antakia is so beautiful a resort that you purposely did not stay on there. Surely Almighty Allah has not forbidden the nice things of this world upon the virtuous. Allah, the Almighty has said in the Holy *Quran* that the Prophets should take the good and nice things of this world and do good actions. In another place Allah, the Almighty says that the believers should take the good things granted to them and be thankful to their Sustainer (the Almighty God). So on this account it was incumbent upon you that you ought to have allowed the tired *Mujahids* of Islam to take respite and enjoy the good things of the world so that they could be refreshed. You have stated that you are waiting for my orders to enter Duroob - the Byzantine border. In this connection, I am to state that you are the man on the spot while I am an onlooker from far-off. The man at a distance cannot see what a person present on the place can do and see. You are in juxtaposition with the enemy. Your informers are constantly pouring in with information for you — so, if, in your opinion it is proper to enter Duroob, send your contingents there and enter the Byzantine territory along with your army. The hilly tracks should be properly guarded. Trusted Christian Arabs should accompany the army as scouts to guide. If the people of Duroob offer for peace, accept the same and adhere to the terms and conditions of peace to your utmost. You have further stated that the Arabs are desirous to marry the Byzantine women because of their charm and beauty. In my opinion those Arabs not having their wives in Hejaz may marry them and those Arabs who wish to buy them as concubines may be allowed to do so, beaause in this way they can be safe from sexual indulgence. Peace be upon you and upon both of us and Blessings and Bendictions of Allah."

(*Futu-hush-sham Vol. 1, pp. 193-94*).

(53)

TO HERACLIUS

After the conquest of Antakia, Hadrat Abu 'Ubaidah bin Jarrah (R.A.A.) sent several contingents towards Byzantine boarders - Duroob-who inflicted heavy losses upon the Byzantines and much booty fell into the hands of the victors: but a military Officer, Hadrat Abdullah bin Huzaifah (R.A.A.), a companion of the Prophet of Allah (S.A.W.) who participated in the Battle of Badr was caught by the Byzantines. On receipt of this information the Caliph, 'Umar Farooq (R.A.A.) wrote the following to the Byzantine Qaiser, Heraclius:

In the name of Allah, Most Compassionate and Merciful.

Priase be to Allah - the Cherisher of all worlds, Who has neither wife nor children. God's Blessings and Benedictions be upon His Prophet and Messenger (S.A.W.).

On receipt of this letter from 'Umar bin Khattab - the Commander of the Faithful return the captive who is under your custody whose name is (Hadrat) Abdullah bin Huzaifah (R.A.A.). If you do so, it is likely that you will receive guidance otherwise I will send a force of the brave whom mercantile or worldly affairs do not keep away from the rememberance of Almighty Allah."

(*Futu-hush-sham, Vol. 3, pp. 161-162*).

(54)

Heraclius wrote to Hadrat 'Umar Farooq (R.A.A.) that his ambassadors returned to him after their meeting with the Caliph in Islam, 'Umar Farooq (R.A.A.). They told him that a strange tree (Date tree) is grown in your country whose big leaves are akin to the ears of an ass, thereafter pearl like white bunches appear upon the date-trees, became green like, emarald; subsequently they became ripe red like gems and tasty like spaghetti when dried up, and serve the purpose of food in time of contingency for the residents and food for the travellers in journey. If my ambassadors are true, certainly this is tree of Paradise.

Hadrat 'Umar Farooq (R.A.A.) replied the following: "From the servant of Allah - 'Umar - the Commander of the Faithful to the Qaiser of Rome.

Your ambassdors have spoken the truth. This is the tree which grow in our country and the same was grown upon Maryam (Mary A.S.) when Hadrat Esa (Jesus Christ A.S.) — was in her womb, Fear Almighty Allah and make not Hadrat Esa (A.S.) the object of worship in juxtaposition to God. Surely, Hadrat Esa (A.S.) is akin to Hadrat Adam (A.S.), who was created out of clay.

"Lo! the likeness of Jesus with Allah is as the likeness of Adam. He created him of dust." (3: 59). (*Seyuti, Tarikhul Khulafa Egypt, 1857*).

(55)

TO HADRAT ABU 'UBAIDAH BIN JARRAH (R.A.A.)

In 17 A.H. Khalid bin Walid (R.A.A.) attacked the Byzantine frontier passes like Duroob under permission and order of Hadrat Abu 'Ubaidah (R.A.A.). During the campaign large booty in the form of wealth fell into the hands of the Mulsims and its news spread far and wide. Hadrat Khalid bin Walid (R.A.A.) reached his head-quarter, Qinsirin. People from far off came to see him and the needy also to receive financial endowments. Among them was also an influential tribal chieftain, Ashas bin Qais. Khalid bin Walid (R.A.A.) gave him an endowment of Ten thousand dirhams. The Caliph, Hadrat 'Umar Farooq (R.A.A.) was annoyed on account of such largesses displayed on the part of Khalid bin Walid (R.A.A.) and wrote the following to Hadrat Abu 'Ubaidah bin Jarrah (R.A.A.)

"After perusal of the contents of my letter, recall Khalid bin Walid (R.A.A.) from Qinsirin to your headquarter, Homs convene public gathering including the whole army, ask Khalid bin Walid (R.A.A.) to stand up to explain his position regarding ten thousand dirhams given to Ashas. If he hesitates to reply, put off his cap and bind him by the rounds of his turban, not sparing him till he tells you from where he got that money. If he admits that the money given to Ashas belonged to the booty fell into the hands of the victors, certainly he is gulity of misappropriation, so realize the money from him post-haste and deposit the same in public treasury. If he takes the plea that it was his personal money, the admission tantamounts that he is spend thrift.

Prodigals are not loved by Allah (7: 31).

Send him to me so that I may punish him for his wasteful conduct."

(*Nasikhut-Tawarikh*, *Vol. 4 p. 347*).

(56)

TO THE MUSLIMS OF THE CANTONMENTS

Hadrat Abu 'Ubaidah (R.A.A.) called Hadrat Khalid bin Walid (R.A.A.) to his headquarter at Homs, the plenipotentiary of Hadrat 'Umar Farooq (R.A.A.) questioned Hadrat Khalid bin Walid (R.A.A.) in a public meeting that the money given to Ashas belonged to him or the public treasury. Hadrat Khalid Bin Walid (R.A.A.) remained silent and inspite of the insistence of the emissary of the Caliph 'Umar (R.A.A.) did not break his silence. The Muazzin of the Messenger of Allah (S.A.W.), Hadrat Bilal (R.A.A.), the matured and the aged, fearlessly truthful, was present on the spot, who stood up and said that such are the orders from the Caliph 'Umar (R.A.A.) He put off the cap of Khalid bin Walid (R.A.A.), bound the turban round his neck and asked the same question again. Hadrat Khalid (R.A.A.) replied, "I had given the money as gift from my personal account." Hadrat Bilal (R.A.A.) put on the cap upon the head of Hadrat Khalid (R.A.A.), unfastened the turban and apologized. Hadrat Abu 'Ubaidah bin Jarrah (R.A.A.) could not tell him that Khalid bin Walid (R.A.A.) has been removed from his rank because that might have grieved him. On account of his removal, great agitation, anger and protest was expressed in Iraq and specially in Madina People became restless because of such an insulting and degrading treatment with a general of the army whose flag always remained aloft in the warfare, who rendered matchless service in the cause of Islam and in the establishment of Islamic government. It became necessary for the Caliph "Umar Farooq (R.A.A.) to explain his position before the public regarding the steps taken by him in this direction. So the following was despatched to all the Muslims of the cantonments:

"I have not removed him (Khalid bin Walid R.A.A.) on account of the charge of misappropriation or personal displeasure but because people were enamoured of his conquests,, so I apprehended that people may rely on him instead of Almighty Allah and may entangle themselves in the difficult position of considering Khalid bin Walid (R.A.A.) as the resolver of their difficulties. I wish that people should realize that not Khalid bin Walid (R.A.A.) but, Almighty Allah is the Real Resolver of our problems."

(*Tabari, Vol. 4, pp. 205-206*).

(57)

TO HADRAT ABU 'UBAIDAH BIN JARRAH (R.A.A.)

In 18 A.H. Hadrat Abu 'Ubaidah bin Jarrah (R.A.A.) informed the Caliph, 'Umar Farooq (R.A.A.), that a group of the companions of the Messenger of Allah (S.A.W.) were found guilty of drinking wine and argue on the basis of the Quranic verse (5. 91) that drinking of wine is not proved to be prohibited. Hadrat 'Umar Farooq (R.A.A.) wrote the following:

"Call these people, if they believe that wine is permissible, they should be killed and if they believe in its prohib..ion, they should be given eighty stripes per head."

(*Tabari, Vol. 4, p. 222*).

(58)

TO HADRAT ABU HANZAL (R.A.A.)

In compliance of the orders of the Caliph, Hadrat Abu 'Ubaidah bin Jarrah (R.A.A.) called the companions of the Messenger of Allah (S.A.W.) who were found guilty of drinking wine and questioned them whether wine is prohibited or not. They all replied in the affirmative that the drinking of wine is unlawful and prohibited. Everyone of them was given eighty leashes. They were so ashamed of their mistake that they hid their faces in their houses and never came out. Abu Hanzal (R.A.A.) was supra-sensitive, so he lost his balance of mind. The matter was brought to the notice of the Caliph in Islam, 'Umar Farooq (R.A.A.) by the Commander-in-Chief of the forces in Syria, Abu 'Ubaidah bin Jarrah (R.A.A.) with a recommendatary letter for Abu Hanzal (R.A.A.) for consolation from the Caliph who wrote the following:

"From 'Umar (R.A.A.) to Abu Hanzal (R.A.A.).
Allah pardonth not that partners should be ascribed unto Him". (4:48)

Commissions of sins of lesser degree may be forgiven by Allah, if He Wills: So you repent, raise your head, come out in the open and do not be disappointed as Allah, the Almighty says in the Quran:

'O My slaves who have been prodigal to their own hurt! Despair not of the mercy of Allah, Who forgiveth all sins. Lo! He is the Forgiving, the Merciful." (39:53)

(*Tabari, Vol. 4, p. 222*).

(59)

TO THE MUSLIMS

It was brought to the notice of Hadrat 'Umar Farooq (R.A.A.) that the balance of mind of those companions who drank wine had been upset on account of the fact that the Mulsims in general used to curse them off and on, they hid themselves in their houses; so the Caliph 'Umar Farooq (R.A.A.) despatched the following instructions to the common Muslims in that regard:

"You should keep your eyes on your own doings ; if someone acts unlawful he should be taken to task but none should curse him otherwise you will be put into unseen trouble."

(*Tabari, Vol. 4, p. 223*).

(60)

TO HADRAT ABU 'UBAIDAH BIN JARRAH (R.A.A.)

There are some variations regarding the details in the matter of Hadrat Abu Jandal's drinking, on the authority of Ibn-i-Abdul-Birr Andulusi in his book *'Isti aab* as reported by Abdur-Razzaq. According to these reports and details available in the references cited above, there were two other participants namely. Hadrat Darraar bin Khattab and Hadrat Abu Zarr (R.A.A.) along with Hadrat Abu Jandal (R.A.A.) When Hadrat Abu 'Ubaidah bin Jarrah (R.A.A.) questioned them on the Issue. Hadrat Abu Jandal (R.A.A.) cited the following verse of the Quran to affirm the permissible attitude towards wine.

"There shall be no sin (imputed) unto those who believe and do good works for what they have eaten (in the past). So be mindful of your duty (to Allah) and do good works (5:93).

(61)

While informing the Caliph about Abu Jandal (R.A.A.) regarding his drinking of wine, Hadrat Abu 'Ubaidah bin Jarrah (R.A.A.) also complained to the Caliph 'Umar Farooq (R.A.A.) that Abu Jandal (R.A.A.) tried to shut his mouth by means of the above cited verse of the Quran. So 'Umar Farooq (R.A.A.) wrote the following:

"The Satan who made this crime (Drinking) of wine pleasant in the eyes of Abu Jandal (R.A.A.) the same had presented it in a sophisticated manner before him. So you go ahead with the award of punishment prescribed for it."

(62)

TO HADRAT ABU JANDAL (R.A.A.)

On hearing the enforcement of Divine Law (Hadd) regarding award of punishment all the three - Hadrat Abu Zarr, Darrar and Abu Jandal (R.A.A.) became excited. Hadrat Abu Zarr (R.A.A.) said that they should be given time for a day as they intend to go for Jihad; if they are killed in action well and good but if they survive the prescribed punishment for drinking may be enforced on them. All the three went out for Jehad, Hadrat Abu Zarr (R.A.A.) was killed in action while the other two - Hadrat Darrar and Abu Jandal (R.A.A.) were awarded the prescribed punishment, who said at that time that lie was ruined. Hadrat Abu 'Ubaidah (R.A.A.), mentioned the above words from Abu Jandal (R.A.A.) while sending his report in despatch to the Caliph 'Umar Farooq (R.A.A.) who wrote the following to Abu Jandal (R.A.A.):

"The real Satan who presented this sin handsomely before Abu Jandal (R.A.A.) the same also kept him (Abu Jandal R.A.A.) out from repenting. . . .

"Ha Mim. The revelation of the scripture is from Allah the Mighty, the Knower The Forgiver of Sin, the

Accepter of repentance, the Stern in punishment, the Bountiful. (40: 1 to 3)

(*Isti-aab Ibn Abdul Birr, Hyderabd (India), 1336 A.H. Vol. 2, p. 632-33*).

(63)

TO HADRAT ABU 'UBAIDAH BIN JARRAH (R.A.A.)

In 18 A.H. plague overtook Syria, having its start from Amwas, a town near Jerusalem. According to reasonable calculated estimates twenty five thousand Muslims died, on account of plague, comprising many companions of the Prophet of Allah, who died in the epidemic including, the Commander-in-Chief, Hadrat Abu 'Ubaidah bin Jarrah (R.A.A.), his advisers, Hadrat Mu'aaz bin Jabal, Hadrat Yazid bin Abi Sufyan and Hadrat Shuraih-beel bin Hasanah (R.A.A.) are some of the distinguished personalities. It is stated that Hadrat Abu 'Ubaidah bin Jarrah and Mu'aaz bin Jabal (R.A.A.) believed in pre-determinism and were pleased in its execution so they considered unnecessary to seek an asylum against the general spread of plague. Hadrat 'Umar Farooq (R.A.A.) believed otherwise. When the Caliph 'Umar Farooq (R.A.A.) came to know that Abu Ubaidah bin Jarrah (R.A.A.) is not ready to proceed to a safer place or to leave Syria (plague-stricken area) he wrote the following in order to take him out of the impending peril:

"Peace be on you. There is an impending problem and I want to talk to you in person. Consider it as prime expediency, do not leave the letter from your hand till you start."

((*Tabari, Vol. 4, p. 201*).

(64)

Hadrat Abu 'Ubaidah (R.A.A.) caught the Caliph's point and apologised that he was the Commander-in-Chief of the Muslims in Syria, therefore it does not seem proper that he may leave the Muslims in this hour of calamity and should not be forced to come at the head-quarter. There are different reactions of the Caliph 'Umar Farooq (R.A.A.) as reported by the historians. On receipt of the letter from Hadrat Abu 'Ubaidah (R.A.A.) tears fell down from the Caliph 'Umar's (R.A.A.) eyes. People asked whether the Commander-in-Chief Abu 'Ubaidah (R.A.A.) passed away from this world. He replied, not yet, but we should take it so, and sent the followig despatch:

"Peace be on you. It is a steepy place where you have encamped the Muslims. Take them to a higher, neat and clean place."

(*Tabari, Vol. 4, p. 201*).

According to another version reported in *Lisaanul-Arab* and *Kanzul 'Ummal*, Hadrat 'Umar Farooq (R.A.A.) stated that Jordon where he had stationed the Muslims is damp and calamity stricken area; on the contrary Jaabiyah is a neat, clean and healthy resort; therefore take the Muslims there.

(65)

TO HADRAT ABU 'UBAIDAH BIN JARRAH (R.A.A.)

Different dates have been assigned by the Arab narrators regarding the conquest of the most vital city of Quisariyah in Syria - 16,18 and 19 or 20 A.H. According to the version of Futu-hush-sham, Hadrat Abu 'Ubaidah bin Jarrah (R.A.A.) remained alive after the conquest of Syria in 19 A.H. so the letter may be studied in this context in view of the authority stated above. The glad tiding of the conqeust of Qaisaariyah were despatched to the Caliph 'Umar Farooq (R.A.A.) through a person, clad in gaudy clothes that fell booty into the hands of the Muslims as a result of Byzantine defeat. The Caliph was grieved to see the person dressed in such clothes, and also came to know that Muslims had been addicted to the pleasures of this mundane world in preference to the niceities and blessings of the hereafter, so the following despatch to the Commander of the forces in Syria, Hazrat 'Ubaidah bin Jarrah (R.A.A.)

"In the name of Allah, All Compassionate and Most Merciful.

From the servant of Allah, 'Umar bin Khattab (R.A.A.) to Abu Ubaidah bin Jarrah (R.A.A.).

I am grateful to Almighty Allah, except Whom there is none worthy of worship and send blessings and benedictions upon His Prophet Muhammad (S.A.W.) I am pleased to know that Almighty Allah graced the Muslims with the grand victory and bestowed upon them the treasures of Qaiser as promised by our beloved Prophet and Messenger of Allah (S.A.W.). Soon the treasuries of the Kisra will also come into the hands of the Muslims. Side by side it has come to my notice that the Arab Bedouins of the army are being enticed by the worldly pleasures of life, charmed by the fascinations of this life in preference to the palaces and blessings of the Paradise. They walk proudly dressed in gaudy clothes of safun and silk, take wheat bread and pudding, have become negligent of the hereafter due to the worldly taste of the tongue and the body. O Ibn-e-Jarrah (R.A.A.), it has come to my notice that they have become unmindful of Salat - the five times obligatory prayer in Islam and other obligations sanctioned in *Deen-Islam.* Teach them a lesson by sending a pure, Arab breed horse contingent of the army: be strict instead of being lenient upon their waywardness due to slackness, otherwise they will be after you and harm you. Anyone deviating from the lawful obligations of Islam should be punished without fear or favour. You should remember that you have been entrusted to be the officer of the people and are answerable to Allah regarding their waywardiiness. Almighty Allah says that He will grant leadership to those who will establish Salat, pay the poor due (Zakat), enjoin the good deeds and forbid the wrong. The Messenger of Allah, Muhammad (S.A.W.) has said about you that Abu 'Ubaidah (R.A.A) is the custodian of the Muslim sunnah; so discharge your responsibility in the matter of being the custodian of the people. Whoso does not offer *Salat* or obligatory prayer do punish him. Whenever the Messenger of Allah (S.A.W.) and ourselves were in conversation and prayer time approached, we used to be absorbed in our prayers as if we do not know each other. Again the Messenger of Allah said: Almighty Allah has enjoined mosques to be His abode and also the people worshipping in the mosques are His guests. Really the person is fortunate who goes to a place to see Me after proper purification so it is incumbent upon Me as his Host to show proper regard and respect to the person concerned. The Messenger of Allah (S.A.W.) further declared: All obligations (Faraaiz) are incumbent upon me till I am in this world but Salat is an obligation enjoined to be performed even in the heavans.

On receipt of my letter ask 'Amr bin Aas to march with his army and keep the learned Companions like Hadrat Asmir bin Rabeea in the fore-front. Apart from this despatch the force available to conquer the territory of Rabeea and Judd bin Saalih i.e. Mesopotamiya. It is my earnest prayer to Allah that He may help you And Peace and Blessings of Allah be upon you."

(*Futu-hush-Sham , Vol. 2, pp. 56-57*).

(66)

TO HADRAT ABU UBAIDAH BIN JARRAH (R.A.A.)

The letter reproduced below seems to have been addressed to the above named companion of the Prophet of Allah (S.A.W.) in 20 A.H., according to the version of Futu-hush-sham.

In the name of Allah, the Beneficent and Most Merciful. Peace and Blessings from the servant of Allah 'Umar the

Commander of the Faithful to Abu 'Ubaidah bin Jarrah (R.A.A.). I am grateful to Almighty Allah except Whom there is none worthy of worship and send my Blessings and Salutations upon His Prophet and Messenger, Muhammad (S.A.W.). You have rendered meritorious services in the cause of the execution of the non-believers - *Kuffaar* - the reward for which will be received by you on the Day of Accountability We have never seen you lacking in the performance of your duty; You remained steadfast on the path of the Prophet (S.A.W.) and served the cause of Islam according to the best of your capacity and ability. Allah Almighty may reward you for your endeavours for the cause of Islam and may forgive your shortcomings. On receipt of this letter of mine send an army under the command of Hadrat Ayaz bin Ghanam in the area of Rebeea and Bakr (Mesopotamiya). I am sanguine that Almighty Exalted Allah will render this land subdued at the hands of Ayaz bin Ghanam. Please instruct 'Ayaz, on my behalf, to be fearful of Allah and do his utmost for His Pleasure. Never show negligence in the matter of *Jihad*. Follow the footsteps of those believers who fought in the cause of Allah and adhered to the commandment of Allah revealed on the Messenger of Allah, Muhammad (S.A.W.) in the Quran:

> "O Prophet! strive against the disbelievers and the hypocrites." (9: 73)

Peace and Blessings be upon you and all Muslims."

(*Futu-hush-sham, Vol. 2, pp. 56-57*).

(67)

TO HADRAT YAZID BIN ABI SUFAYAN (R.A.A.)

In 18 A.H. Hadrat Abu 'Ubaidah bin Jarrah (R.A.A.) died of plague and appointed his adviser Hadarat Mu'aaz bin Jabal (R.A.A.), as his successor at the time of his death. A few days later he also fell victim of plague spreading in the epidemic form who appointed Hadrat Amar bin 'Aas as his successor, but the Caliph, 'Umar

Farooq (R.A.A.) selected the son of Abu Sufyan, Hadrat Yazid (R.A.A.) as the supreme Commander of the Muslim forces and despatched the following letter to him:

"Be it known to you that I have appointed you as the Supreme Commander of the entire Syrian forces and ordered th whole army to follow your orders and never to ignore your insight in any matter. March towards Qaisariyah as soon as possible and continue its seige till it is subdued. Syrian conquest cannot be fully utilized until the Byzantine inhabitants of Qaisariyah lay their arms before you as they are the real thorn in your side. Besides, not a single soul shall leave the idea of Syria as long as he is faithful subject of Qaiser. If you conquer Qaisariyah their hopes will be cut off from Syria. Consequently I fervently hope that Almighty and Exalted Allah will surely grace the Muslims with the award of the conquest of Qaisriyah

(*Azdi, p. 250*).

(68)

TO THE MILITARY COMMANDERS IN SYRIA

"You are informed that I have appointed Yazid bin Abi Sufyan *R.A.A.) Supreme-in-Command of the forces in Syria and ordered to attack Qaisaariyah. Act according to his orders and acumen. And Peace and Blessings be upon you."

(*Azdi, p. 250*).

(69)

HADRAT YAZID BIN ABI SUFYAN (R.A.A.)

The following letter is being reproduced from *Kanzul-'Ummal*

"Send an army whose flag should be in the hands of a leader from Rabia tribe. I have heard from the Messenger of

Allah (S.A.W.) that the army shall not be defeated whose flag will be in the hands of a Rabia.

(70)

HADRAT YAZID BIN ABI SUFYAN (R.A.A.)

The letter under reference was written after the receipt of information of the conquest of Qaisaariyah, a vital commercial centre in Palestine, situated on the sea-coast, whose formidable fortress could easily stand in comparison with the famous fort of *Haft Khwan.* It was true that the hardest possible resistence was offered to the Muslim as compared to all the cities in Syria. The city was beseiged several times but the guards inside the fort were not subdued, because it was here that the Christians belongings to Byzantine race were settled in large number, whose fidelity to their government, religion and its institutions was far greater than the original inhabitants of Syria. Morever, there was constant flow of necessities of life through sea-route so the conquest of Qaisaariyah remained an embarrassing practical problem:

"Let it be known that I am in receipt of your letter and am apprised of the local situation through its contents. I am grateful to Exalted Almighty Allah Who has granted us the grand victory of 'Qaisairiyah in Syria. All Priase is for Allah that He has bestowed upon us satisfaction through this conquest, new vistas of resources are opened, your enemies have been humiliated and your aspirations have come to realization. Be thankful to Almighty Allah for the graces conferred upon you because the graces and blessings are increased due to thanksgiving and the eternal grace of success is perpetuated.

"If ye would count the bounty of Allah ye cannot reckon it. (-14: 34).

(71)

TO HADRAT 'AYAZ BIN GHANAM (R.A.A.)

As already stated that according to one school of thought among the Arab narratorrs, Hadrat 'Abu 'Ubaidah bin Jarrah (R.A.A.) had nominated Hadrat Muaaz bin Jabal (R.A.A.) his successor at his death bed, and he had appointed Hadrat 'Umar bin 'Aas (R.A.A.) after a few days as he also fell a victim to plague. Acording to another school of historical narrators, Hadrat Abu 'Ubaidah bin Jarrah (R.A.A.) had nominated Hadrat 'Ayaz bin Ghanam (R.A.A.) his successor as he was his relation, adviser and a great commander of Muslim forces, whose action was duly supported by Hadrat 'Umar Farooq (R.A.A.) and ratified the same through the following letter:

"I appoint you governor of all those territories held under the control of Hadrat Abu 'Ubaidah (R.A.A.). Do your duty nicely and diligently."

(Ibn-Sa'd, Tabaqat, Vol. 7, pp. 122)

(72)

TO HADRAT 'AYAZ BIN GHANAM (R.A.A.)

"Peace and Blessings from the servant of Allah, Umar, (R.A.A.), Commander of the faithful, to 'Ayaz bin Ghanam (R.A.A.).

We have always found you absorbed in leading different expeditions and conducting negotiations on behalf of the Muslims, and you have always been busy in exhorting the Muslims to lead virtuous life. This had also been the practice of your forefathers. I convey to you glad tidings of the Divine reward and blissful ending of this world and the Hereafter as you are adorned with the good qualities of head and heart. I fervently hope, God Willing, you will succeed in this world and your good name shall be perpetuated. I think you must be knowing that the elders of Byzantine have collected huge armies in the Jazira. I wish to send an army that may disperse them, whose commander should be brave, wise, well-versed in warfare and God-fearing. I considered the matter myself and also consulted the distinguished companions (R.A.A.) and came to the conclusion that the expedition should be entrusted to you as no other better person is available to accomplish it. After going through the letter, you may ask the Commander-in-Chief of the Syrian forces, Hadrat Yazid bin Abi Sufyan (R.A.A.), to place at your disposal the force you may consider necessary and march towards Jazira Your deportment should be the fear of Allah, Who knows your interior and exterior self both. Whatever problems come before you, decide them according to the Quraan, if their solution is not found in the Quraan refer them to the practice and precept of the Prophet Muhammad (S.A.W.) and Hadrat Abu Bakr (R.A.A.); do not be disheartened on account of the heavy majority in number of the enemy and your scarcity in men and money. The force of Islam was less in number in many expeditions, but ultimately was successful. You must have heard that the Prophet of Allah (S.A.W.) had declared before us on the occasion of the Battle of Ditch that the day is not far off when Almighty Allah will grant you victory over the territories of the Qaiser and Kisra at your hands and will benefit you through their wealth. Ayaz! You must have seen that Almighty Allah made the prophecy of the Prophet (S.A.W.) a living reality and the territories of Qaisar and Kisra were placed at our disposal. The disbelievers were defeated and capitvated at the hands of the Muslims. Everyone of them accepted our superiority and agreed to pay Jiziyah, the King of the disbelievers, Heraclius ran away in fear to Constantinople - all this is due to the Grace and Blessings of Allah and it is incumbent on us to be grateful to Him.

> That is the bounty of Allah; which He giveth unto whom He will. Surely Allah is of infinite bounty. Al-
> (*Al-Quran, 62: 4*)

I have written to Yazid bin Abi Sufyan (R.A.A.) separately to send the requisite force needed by you for the expedition in Jazirah to be used against Byzantines to settle account with them and march on to *Jazirah* with the Blessings of Allah and engage yourself whole heartedly in the completion of the expedition.

(*Ibn, A'sim p. 56*).

(73)

TO HADRAT 'AYAZ BIN GHANAM

The letter under reference is to be found in the annals of Syria by Ibn-'Asaakir. As regards with reference to its context, it is based upon certain presumptions due to certain ambiguities as evidenced from the preface of the book concluding that no regular rate of revenue was fixed by Hazrat 'Ayaz (R.A.A') in Jazirah, but the same depended upon the principle as the weather permit the fertility of the soil and yield of the crop. Due to the attack by the Muslims, there was disturbance among the population, therefore, the crop could not yield in time. There was delay in revenue to be sent to Madina as the rate of revenue could not be fixed in many places. Therefore, the Caliph in Islam, 'Umar Farooq (R.A.A.) wrote the following:

"You have been late in remitting the revenues although its importance is fully known to you, the main source to wage Jihad against the enemy as well as the basic means of subsistance of the Muslims including myself. In view of it, realize the revenue promptly and despatch the same post-haste without undue hardship or leniency to the tenants.

(*Ibn 'Asakir*)

(74)

TO HADRAT 'AYAZ BIN GHANAM (R.A.A.)

Peace and Blessings from the Servant of Allah, 'Umar, the Commander of the Believers, to 'Ayaz, bin Ghanam.

I am grateful to Almighty Allah, Who got the Jazirah conquered at the hands of the Muslims, changed their diversity into welfare and opened new vistas of livelihood: Now I am not afraid of their diversity or poverty but I feel apprehension that they might become proud due to abundance of wealth and thus be ruined. May Almighty Allah reward you on account of the continuous efforts made by you for the completion of the successful expedition of the Jazirah, the good policy adopted by you for the cause of Islam and the Muslims. On going through this letter, appoint a governor for Jazirah from among the army in whom you could confide in the matter of his words and deeds and return to Syria as early as possible because the Commander-in-Chief in Syria, Hadrat Abi Sufyan (R.A.A.) is seriously ill and if he breathes his last before your arrival in Syria, I apprehend that the country may be lost and Muslim solidarity be scattered. Therefore, leave Jazirah at once, without loss of time. Peace and Blessings be upon you.

(*Ibn-'Asakir*)

(75)

TO HADRAT MUAWIYAH BIN ABI SUFYAN (R.A.A.)

After his return from Jazirah, Ayaz (R.A.A.) reached his headquarter in Syria, Homs; but he fell ill and died: Hadrat Yazid bin Abi Sufyan (R.A.A.) was also suffering seriously in his Syrian headquarter, Damascus. who also died in 18 A.H. According to the version of Buladuri, thus leaving Hadrat Muawiyah (R.A.A.) all alone to the Syrian front, who was on account of his constant application, hard labour, peneterating understanding, marching on in high position from one stage to another. Being impressed by his services Caliph 'Umar Farooq (R.A.A.) appointed him as the Commander-in-Chief of the Syrian forces after the demise of Yazid (R.A.A.). Muawiyah (R.A.A.) had already conquered Qaisariyah. After assuming charge of his post. Amir Muawiyah conquered the coastal cities that were still in the possession of the Byzantines:

"*In the name of Allah, the Beneficent, the Merciful.*

From the bondman of Allah, 'Umar, the Commander of the Believers to Muawiyah bin Abi Sufyan.

You must know that Almighty Allah fulfilled His promise, humiliated the polytheists and established the dominence of Islam. The Messenger of Allah, Muhammad (S.A.W.) prophesied to his (S.A.W.) Ummah the conquest of Syria and other countires - the same has come out true including the good tidings of gaining the possessions and treasuries of the tyrants that fell into the hands of the Muslim victors. Amongst them the most vital is the conquest of Qaisariyah whose fortress enjoyed unique position with regard to its formidable nature and was considered to be impregnable by the Byzantines. Now it is imperative to pay heed to Ghazah, Asqalan (Ports) and the adjoining settlements. The Messenger of Allah (S.A.W.) had declared:

"You will obtain victories in Syria and I give you good news of the two brides i.e. Ghazah and the Asqalaan.

The time is not far off when the Muslims will be rehabilitated on the Sea-Coast. When the civil war starts in the East and West and residence becomes difficult in the cities as well as the towns, you should settle yourself in Asqalan. Further there is a good part of every thing and the good portion of Syria is her city of Asqalaan. After going through the contents of this letter, you should at once march on Asqalaan and make every possible effort to redeem the same as well as adjoining areas from the Byzantine power. It is fervently prayed for and hoped that this nice city with its suburbs will surely be conquered through your hands by the Grace of Almighty Allah. Do inform me daily of the occurrences and local events after reaching Asqalaan and peace and blessings be upon you."

(*Ibn A'sim p. 6*).

(76)

TO HADRAT MUAWIAYAB BIN ABI SUFYAN (R.A.A.)

When Hadrat Amir Muawiyah (R.A.A.) conquered the Syrian Sea-Coast cities like 'Akka, Sour, Yafa etc., he wrote to the Caliph 'Umar Farooq (R.A.A.) to grant permission to conquer Cyprus as it is so near the Syrian coast that the chirping of its birds is heard. It is extremely fertile and full of natural resources, different varieties of fruits etc. It is easy to gain possession of it. 'Umar Farooq (R.A.A.) wrote to the Governor of Egypt, Hadrat 'Amr bin Aas (R.A.A.), regarding the feasibility of such a voyage, who described the same as extremely perilous and opposed the undertaking of such expedition through sea. So the Caliph 'Umar Farooq (R.A.A.) wrote the following to Amir Muawiyah (R.A.A.).

'Let it be known to you that Almighty Allah has entrusted me the responsibility to look after the *Ummah* of the Prophet Muhammad (S.A.W.) and so seek His help and guidance to discharge the same. I do not consider feasible in any way to allow them to undergo the perils of a dangerous voyage and lay seige upon Cyprus by embarking upon sea-boats. In spite of it, I considered the matter myself and also consulted those experienced in nautical activities who are also of the view that the dangerous expedition should be avoided, so you should leave the idea of this venture and never correspond with me on this topic of undertaking the *Jihad* by sea and Peace be upon you."

(*Ibn-e-A'sim p. 62*).

There are a few versions of the above mentioned letter, deterring Amir Muawiyah (R.A.A.) to undertake such hazardous journey by Sea. Hadrat 'Umar Farooq (R.A.A.), the Caliph, was of the view that the life of one single Muslim individual is more precious than the whole Byzantine Empire.

Another version of the above mentioned letter,

We have heard that there is the largest Ocean of the world in front of the Syrian coast praying day and night to Almighty Allah, that it may not be allowed to flow on the earth so that it may engulf the entire earth. So how can I allow the Muslim army to undertake voyage on such rebellious like disbeliever - the perilous sea. By Allah, the life of one single Muslim is dearer to me than the whole Byzantine empire. Beware ! Never undertake the naval expedition without my express command, the permission for the same is forbidden. Never disobey in this regard otherwise you know the punishment awarded to Alaa Hadrami when he undetook expedition (Southern Faris) without my permission."

(*Tabari Vol. 5, p. 52*).

(77)

TO THE BYZANTINE EMPEROR

All the undermentioned four letters were addressed to the Byzantine Emperor most porbably after the capitulation of Qaisariyah in 18 A.H., the last stronghold of the Byzantines is Syria. After its fall, the Byzantine Qaiser gave up his aggressive activities and desired to establish friendly relations with Madinah. Some Arabic narrators and writers state that the Byzantine Emperor requested the Caliph, 'Umar Farooq (R.A.A.) to send him a few words comprehensive enough to contain all that is required, who worte the following:

"Wish for your subjects the same that you wisn for yourself, do not like that for your subject which you do not like for yourselves. If you will act upon it, you will be the master of wisdom. Try to comprehend those who are not before you on the basis of those who are with you, thus your circle of acquaintance will be widened."

(*Tabari, Vol, 5, p. 52*).

(78)

On second occasion, the Byzantine Qaiser sent a bottle and requested the Caliph, 'Umar Farooq (R.A.A.) to fill it with that which is everything in this world. Hadrat 'Umar Farooq (R.A.A.) filled it with water and stated:

"This (water) is evertything in this world."

(*Tabari*, *Vol. 5, p. 52*).

(79)

The next embassy from Constantinople (Istanbul) brought this question. What is the difference between truth and falsehood? Hadrat 'Umar Farooq (R.A.A.) replied the following:

(As the distance among) four fingers: whatever you see with your eyes is called truth and whatever cannot be experienced through the eyes and are based upon mere hearsay are generally fase."

(*Tabari 1, Vol. 5, p. 52*).

(80)

Once the Qaiser asked about the traversing time between East and West and earth and the heaven. The Caliph 'Umar Farooq (R.A.A.) wrote:

"If the path is clear and thorough, a traveller can accompish the same in five hundred years."

(*Tabari*, *Vol. 5, p. 52*).

(81)

TO HADRAT MUAWIYAH BIN ABI SUFYAN (R.A.A.)

"Do not hide yourself from the people. Permit the poor to see you. treat him with kindness so that he may express himself freely and be encouraged. Take special care for the stranger and foreigner because if he is made to stay long for the settlement of his case, he will be disgusted and annoyed. Thus discouraged he will return and go away without getting his due right."

(*Izalatul-Khifa, Vol. 2, p. 182*).

(82)

TO HADRAT MUAWIYAH BIN ABI SUFYAN (R.A.A.)

"Be steadfast while traversing on the path of truth. If you do so Almighty Allah will show to you all the stages of the truthful. Keep truth and justice before you while deciding everything."

(*Kanzul-'Ummaal, Vol. 8, p. 200*).

(83)

TO HADRAT SAEED BIN 'AAMIR HAZIM (R.A.A.)

The letter under discussion was received during the Seige of Qarqaisaa' a city of Jazirah. The contents of the letter ran thus:

If a slave or a free person of yours grants protection to an individual of the enemy, he will be in your safe custody till you take him to a place of safety or hand him over in his area. If you have forbidden to grant protection to any member of the family of the enemy, but some one amongst you does so on the ground that he did not know that you passed such orders, or he has forgotten, or he has deliberately disobeyed your orders, in any case you cannot inflict any kind of injury to an individual of the enemy. You must take him to a place of safety else he wishes to be with you. Do not commit the least excess to the slave. Servants of Allah because, without the least shadow of doubt you are the soldier of Allah. I f a Muslim points out a particular person to come to him to fight and he, without understanding its full implications, comes to him, even then you cannot harm provided you are satisfied that he has come to you on account of your calling him. But if you are in doubt that he has come due to your pointer and if you are not sure that he has come on his own accord, then it is not necessary to retun him to a place of safety, but make him a *Zimmi* and realize *Jiziyah* from him. If an outsider did not disclose his identity in the camp, catch hold of him, do not provide shelter to him nor render him a *Zimmi:* in such a case you are free to decide whatever you think to be in the general Muslim interest."

(*Mudaw-wa-natul-Kub-ra, Vol. 1, p. 401*).

(84)

TO 'UMAR BIN SA'D ANSARI (R.A.A.)

Hadrat 'Ayaz bin Ghanam (R.A.A.), after conquering Jazirah, while on his way to take charge of the post of Commander-in-Chief of Syria from Hadrat Yazid bin Abi Sufyan (R.A.A.) died in his headquarter at Homs. The Command of Syrian forces was entrusted by the Commander of the faithful, Khalifa, to the younger brother of Yazid, Hadrat Amir Muawiyah (R.A.A.) and appointed a companion of the Prophet of Allah (S.A.W.), Hadrat Saeed bin Aamir bin Huzaim who also died after a short period and was succeeded by 'Umair bin Sa'd (R.A.A.), a distinguished commander of the forces of Hadrat 'Ayaz bin Ghanam (R.A.A.) in Jazirah. Hadrat 'Umar Farooq (R.A.A.) wrote to him:

"The Muslims of your jurisdiction should be ordered to make their slaves makaatib (free after paying the amount). They (the slaves) should be told to provide freedom money even through begging."

(*Kanzul-'Ummaal Vol. 5, p. 255*).

(85)

TO HADRAT UMAIR BIN SA'D (R.A.A.)

One complete year passed after the assumption of the governorship of Homs by Umair bin Sad (R.A.A.), who did not wirte to the Khalifa nor sent the state revenue in the form of (Jiziyah, revenue, Zakat etc.). Certain misgivings arose in the mind of the Khalifa, who wrote the following:

"Come post-haste after perusal of the letter with whatever State income collected as revenue, *Jiziyah*, Zakat etc."

(*Iza-latul-Khifa Vol. II p. 203*).

There is identical version of the letter in *Kanzul-'Ummal.*

(86)

TO THE PEOPLE OF RU'ASH

In the name of Allah, the Beneficent, Most Merciful.

Peace and Blessings of Alalh be upon the inhabitants of Ru'aash from the Commander of the faithful 'Umar (R.A.A.) I am grateful to Almighty Allah except Whom there is none worthy of worship. You had undertaken to become Muslims but subsequently turned renegade. Whoso apologises from apostasy adopts the right way of life, no punishment shall be inflicted upon him and will be well-looked after - remember this and be saved form ruin. Those of you accepting Islam should feel gratified and happy. Whoso from Najran sticks to Christianity, he will be deprived of the protection of Islam in Najrain after the last third portion of the month of Ramadan. Be it clear that Ya 'la (governor of Yemen) has written me that none has been compelled to accept Islam, nor has been coerced and beaten to do so as he has not been allowed to do so under intimidation. I have ordered Ya 'la to realize half of the revenue of the produce imposed. I shall never turn you out till your behaviour and conduct remains intact in a right way".

(*Ibn Salam, p. 99*).

In fact Ru'aash is one of the fertile valleys of Najran and it appears that from Ru 'aash is meant the tribe of Haris bin Ka'b,, who had become Muslim in 10 A.H. at the hands of the forces sent by the Messenger of Allah, Muhammad (S.A.W.) The same turned apostate from Islam and rebels to Madinah after the demise of the Prophet of Allah (S.A.W.). Some historians has stated that the addressees in the letter under reference are the Christians of Najran. This view is incorrect as these Christians never accepted Islam, so the question of their turning renegade from Islam does not arise.

(87)

TO YA 'LA BIN UMMAYYAH

"Take hold of the entire land under the state control that has been taken possession by the exiled persons. The uncultivated land that can be watered through hedging or bonds or having date-gardens etc. may be given away to the Muslims of Najran, so that they may be in a position to lookafter them. Two-third of the produce of the gardens should be realized for the Central state-treasury and one third to be left over to the cultivators. If the gardens are watered from the wells etc., then the produce of the same shall be given two third to the persons cultivating the gardens and one-third shall be remitted to the central state treasury. The uncultivated lands whose watering depends upon hedging or rain may be given to the Muslims of th Najran - its two-third of the produce belongs to the central state-treasury but if the land is watered through buckets then the two-third belongs to the cultivators and one-third to the State Treasury."

(*Abu Yusuf* , *Kitab-ul-Kharaj, p. 75*).

(88)

TO THE GOVERNOR OF SYRIA AND IRAQ

According to Arabic history, three causes are mentioned leading to the exile of the Najrani Christians:

(i) The Messenger of Allah; Muahmmad (S.A.W.) had ordered on his death-bed that none except Islam should be allowed to remain in Arabia as a system of life,

(ii) One of the conditions of the covenant with the Prophet of Allah (S.A.W.) was that the Christians in Najran will no more induige in the forbidden custom of usuary; but after complying with the above for a few years on the above cited stipulation, again started the business through usury (interest) during the *Khilafat* of Hadrat 'Umar Farooq (R.A.A.),

(iii) By this time they had grown in formidable (large) number, collected arms and ammunition so much, so that they posed a threat to the Muslims in Yemen and the State in Madina. So the following letter was sent from the *Khalifa Amirul-Momineen Hadrat 'Umar (R.A.A.)* to the Christians in Najran:

"In the name of Allah, the Beneficent, the Merciful.

This document has been written by Amirul Momineen, 'Umar (R.A.A.) for the people of Najran. Whoso among them leaves his home, they will be under the protection of Allah. No Muslim will harm them. Under the convenant executed during the days of Prophet Muhammad (S.A.W.) and Hadrat Abu Bakr (R.A.A.), be it clear that whoso Christian from Najran goes to the officers in Iraq and Syria, they will give to such Christians land for cultivation. As a result whatever land cultivated by them, they will become owner of such land in lieu of the cultivable lands left over by them in Najran. No one is authorized to prevent them to cultivate such land, sowing the seed therein and having it under the use and possession and none of them will claim any financial revenue. If any Muslim commits any excesses upon them, the Muslims on the spot should rise in favour of the Christians of Najran as they have come under our protection. No levy of Jiziyah upon them during the twenty four months of their new settlement. They will be asked to pay revenue only of the land cultivated by them and this will be without any injustice."

The last portion of the letter under reference seems to be an additon of the later narrators, as there is no mention of any revenue in the agreement executed between the Prophet and Messenger of Allah, Muhammad (S.A.W.) and the Christians of Najran.

There is another version of the letter speaking in the same strain that the Christians of Najran should be given land that could be cultivated by them in lieu of the land abandoned by them. This should be done in the name of God involving their pleasure also.

(89)

TO HADRAT YA 'LA BIN UMMAYYAH

The husband of a woman in Sun 'aa, the Capital of Yemen, proceeded on a journey never to return. The woman had developed relations with some influential persons of Yemen. She had one son also. Fearing that the elderly son may not be source of leaking the information of the secret meetings between the influential people of Yemen and the woman involved, the son was murdered and his dead body was thrown in a desolate well in the city of Sun'a. The concerned woman reported the matter to Ya'la bin Ummayah (R.A.A.), the governor of Yemen, informing him that her son is not traceable. Hadrat Ya 'la (R.A.A.) addressed a public meeting in this regard, requesting them to trace the boy and bring him. A person happened to pass that well, who saw many blue bees coming in and going out of the same. When he peeped into it, he could not bear its stinking smell and thus reported the matter to Ya 'la (R.A.A.) suspecting that the boy is lying dead in the well. People were asked to go down into the well and the dead body of the boy was thus found. The criminals admitted their crime of murder including the reporting woman who accepted her guilt to be an accomplice in the conspiracy hatched up for the purpose. The entire matter was reported to the Khalifa in Madinah, who wrote:

"Those found guilty as accomplices in the assassination should be killed. If all the inhabitants of Sun'a committed the crime of conspiring in the murder, surely I would have killed all the inhabitants of Sun'aa."

(90)

TO HADRAT YA 'LA BIN UMMAYAH (R.A.A.)

In Yemen there are many perfume producing articles, one of them is amber. This was found to be gathered in abundance in between the coastal sea of Aden and Mukhaa. A person found in abundance the amber from the above place. After knowing it, the governor could not decide whether tax should be levied on it or not. The matter was referred to the Caliph, who replied as under:

"Amber is a God given gift, therefore whatever comes out from the sea one fifth should be realized as tax including amber."

Note : The above is reported on the authority of *Kitabul-Kharaaj by Imam Abu Yusuf*. In *Kitabul-Am-waal* by *Qasim bin Salaam* it is stated that one-tenth of such produce should be taken as cess.

(91)

TO HADRAT SUFYAN (R.A.A.) BIN ABDULLAH SAQAFI (R.A.A.)

According to Islamic Law the prohibitions in relationships are equally applicable to those who came under the sucking category of the persons concerned. The governor of Ta'if sought clarification on the legal issues arising out of the same from Hadrat 'Umar Farooq (R.A.A.) who wrote the following:

"If a woman intending to harm two persons from entering into marital relations deprives them from such privilege by giving them facility to suck her own milk from her bosom or a child sucks the milk left over by her from her bosom or a person sucks only once from her bosom, under these (three above mentioned) conditions, prohibition shall not be imposed."

(*Abu Yusuf*, *Kitabul-Kharaaj*, *p. 55*).

EXPEDITIONS RELATING TO FRONTIERS IN IRAQ AND PERSIA.

(92)

TO HADRAT MUSANNA BIN HAARISA (R.A.A.) AND OTHER COMMANDERS

According to Saif-bin 'Umar, in 12 A.H. to 13 A.H. during the Caliphate of Hadrat Abu Bakr, Khalid bin Walid (R.A.A.) and his rightful lieutenant, Musanna bin Harisa Shaibani (R.A.A.) had conquered the Persian territory comprising of military Cantonments from Kazima, the coastal city of the Gulf of Basra upto Hira including the lower and the middle portion of Iraq. In 13 A.H. the government at Madina commissioned Khalid bin Walid (R.A.A.) to proceed to the war-front in Syria, so he marched towards Damascus after handing over the charge of the command to his lieutenant Hadrat Musanna. Iran was the centre of strife and political turmoil at that time. There was no central authority as centrifugal forces were on the fore-front and the military officers were controlling all the keys in administration. Taking into consideration the above stated facts, Hadrat Musanna (R.A.A.) resolved to reap the full advantage of the then existing situation, proceeded to see the Caliph Amir-ul-momineen, Hadrat Abu Bakr Siddiq (R.A.A.) at Madina, apprised him of chaotic conditions then prevailing in Iran and obtained permission to launch nn attack on Iraq, then a subsidiary territory of Iran. He also demanded provision for the army of Islam. Subsequently a few days later, Hadrat Abu Bakr (R.A.A.) breathed his last and Hadrat 'Umar Farooq (R.A.A.) succeeded him who prepared an army for the expedition on Iraq and despatched the same under the command of a business man, Abu Obaid, belonging to the famous tribe of Banu Saqif. Hadrat Musanna bin Harisa (R.A.A.) had reached there earlier and carried on forays on the border towns of Tigris and Eupharates. On the arrival of Abu Obaid Saqafi there were successful encounters with the Iranian forces but in the final battle of Yammul-Jisr (the battle of Bridge) fought in the last days of the month of Ramadan 13 A.H, Abu Obaid was killed in action as he did not pay heed to the counsels of his friends and companions. The Muslims were utterly routed and at least four thousand of them were martyred in the battle or drowned in the river. Fortunately, dissensions and disunity had divided the Iranian forces and there was social rift among them due to the unstable political situation prevailing there. So the Muslims continued their attacks upon the enemy and raided the important towns of Baghdad — Saabaat and Takreeb. Thus the danger was hovering over the Iranian capital of Iraq, Madaain. A deputation of the Iraqi aristrocrats waited upon Ferozaan and Rustam — the leaders of the two most important parties. At this time the reigns of government were in the hands of the Queen, Boraan and Rustam was her minister. The deputation had appealed for help to both the sections under whom the loyalty of the people of Iran was divided then. The appeal to save them from Arab invasion was heard with due sympathy. Thereafter, the distinguished military officers held a conference, inter alia discussing the weaknesses in the Iranian administration, decided to select Prince Yazd Gard as their king as he belonged to the race of Kisra. It was further agreed, in view of the Arab impending danger to devote themselves to administration. New military checkposts and cantonments were established in Iraq. Apart from this, anti-Arab propaganda was intensively let loose in the villages of Iraq, resulting in revolt against the Islamic state. These villages were under the control and levy of the Madina and thus the fire of rebellion broke out. Arab revenue officers, stationed in the villages of Iraq, with small contingents, left their places to seek safety else where. In short, the Iranian forces started rising from each side. Under the situation cited above, Musanna had to abandon his forays mustered his scattered forces on the Arabian frontier by encamping in the famous oasis, Zi-qaar. The centre was already aware of the Iranian revolution and their consequent preparations. So Hadrat 'Umar Farooq (R.A.A.) wrote the following to Musanna including other military leaders:

"Get away from the Iranian forces target: prepare military posts on the rivers, canals and springs, beginning in the contiguous areas of the two countries. The Christian tribes (namely Rabee-ah, Mudhar and their allies should accompany you along with their brave people. If they do not agree for military service, exile them from this land. Tell the Arabs that they should be prepared for all eventualities in the same manner as the Iranians have arisen to meet you in the battlefiled."

(*Tabari, Vol. IV, p. 28*).

(93)

TO THE ARAB COMMANDERS

After the coronation ceremony of Yazdgard in Iran, there were visible signs of rebellion of the people in Iraq against the Arabs and the war preparation on a large scale. Hadrat 'Umar Farooq despatched the following urgent letter to the military persons in Arabian peninsula:

"Send me, as soon as possible, through conscription, every person possessing military insight, man of the field of bravery, having weaponary or a horse.

(*Iktifa, p. 366*).

(94)

TO HADRAT SA'D BIN ABI WAQQAS (R.A.A.)

Hadrat Sa'd bin Abi Waqqas (R.A.A.) was a collector of Zakat for a few Arabian tribes at the time Hadrat 'Umar Farooq (R.A.A.) became the Caliph. He tried hard to collect one thousand horsemen armed with weapons in response to the above cited urgent letter from the Caliph. As a reward of the above meritorious service and on the recommendation of some of the Companions of the Prophet of Allah, Muhammad (S.A.W.), Hadrat Sa'd bin Abi Waqqas (R.A.A.) was appointed supreme in command of the forces in Iraq. At the time of march from Madina, there were four thousand fighting persons under his command, majority amongst them belonged to Yemen. Hadrat Sa'd (R.A.A.) had instructions to encamp at Zarood, inviting through persuasion the residing tribes of Tamim, Asad and Ribaab to join against the enemy on the front. The Oasis settlements of Zarood lay situated seven hundred miles from Madina on the Arab-Iraq border, on the skirts of Heerah near the town of Qadsiyah (the place where the famous battle was fought a few month later). A few weeks after the arrival of Hadrat Sa'd at Zarood, eight thousand fighting young men from Tamim, Asad and Ribaab became part and parcel of the Muslim forces under Sa'd bin Abi Waqqas (R.A.A.). During this period, Hadrat Musanna (R.A.A.) almost received a fatal wound that became cancer, so he (R.A.A.) died a few months later and his army of eight thousand men also joined with Sa'd (R.A.A.), then comprising the thirty-five thousand fighting men at Qudsiyah representing the last element of Arab Solidarity nobility and bravery. Hadrat Sa'd (R.A.A.) was encamping at Zarood that he recieved the news of the sad demise of Hadrat Musanna bin Harisa (R.A.A.) He was a man of very strong nerves, capable commander, famous for carrying successful forays in the land of the enemy and thus created havoc and terror into the hearts of the enemy in Iraq. He arranged to bring safely several thousand defeated Muslims at the battle of Jisr — an achievement of outstanding ability and meritorious capability of the Supreme-in-Command of the young Muslims in Iraq. He almost received a fatal wound in the battle of Jisr, which turned into cancer and he died of the same a few months later. The news of his death reached Hadrat 'Umar Farooq (R.A.A.) through Sa'd bin Abi Waqqas ((R.A.A.), who considered further stay of Sa'd (R.A.A.) at Zarood inexpedient and ordered him to march on the frontier of Iraq and thus fill up the vaccum created by the death of Hadrat Musanna (R.A.A.) He was further directed to march towards Sharaf for the complete safety of the Muslims, resulting in the due reform and thus calling the people to Islam. Hadrat Sa'd (R.A.A.) marched towards Sharaf from Zarood and the following despatch was received by him: In fact Sharaf was a halting station at a distance of about hundred miles south of Qadsiyah.

"A Commander with some force, whose appointemnt I leave upon your insight and discretion, be sent to the mouth of Tigris (Furujul-Hind) to create a military post to check the Iranians if they happen to attack the Muslims from that side (*Furujul-Hind*).

(95)

During the period of encampment at Sharaf, the following letter was received by Hadrat Sa'd bin Abi Waqqas (R.A.A.) from the Caliph — Hadrat 'Umar Farooq (R.A.A.).

"On receipt of my letter the Muslim forces should be distributed in ten divisions, appoint a headman (*areef*) over every tenth soldier, a Commander for every division: Organise the entire fighting force on the fashion of war-fare i.e., Right, Left and the Middle. This should be executed under due consultation with the Muslims' leaders: they should be present at the time of formation of the divisions also, thereafter send them to their respective division in due command. Ask them to meet you at the battlefield of Qaudsiyah and call back Mughira bin Sho'ba (R.A.A.). along with his contingent to stay with you. Thereafter, inform me of the planning of the people of Persia."

(*Tabari, Vol. IV, p. 87*).

(96)

"March ahead towards Persia (Qadsiyah) from Sharaf. Trust in Allah and seek His help in all your activities. Remember that you are marching to fight a nation who is superior to you in number and weapons, are brave people and that you are entering a country, considered a plain, yet movement is difficult due to rivers, canals and dark pitched nights. Meet the enemy and attack him whenever you happen to see him without waiting for his attack. Do not indulge into any sort of covnersation or discussion with the enemy. Be careful that the enemy, who is very clever in his manoeuvring may not be able to inflict injury upon you through his planning. The material sources of the enemy are large and you can succeed against the enemy only when you devote whole heartedly to the cause dear to you. When you reach Qadsiyah, the gateway of Iraq for the Iranians during the days of Jahiliyah (Ignorance), where the necessaries of life are far more in existence than through any other route. It is fortified from military point of view and full of resources leading head bridges and canals that are difficult to cross: so you should prepare military check-posts leading to all routes. Please see to it that your army should encamp in the open plain, lying in between the Arabian desert (west) and the population in the East. Be steadfast and firm to your place till the enemy attacks you with full force with all his contingents, soldiers on foot etc., due to the fact that you have harassed the enemy from all sides on account of night attacks and forays. If you could retain patience with all firmness only for the sake of good pleasure of Allah and fight the battle sincerely, I am hopeful that you will be successful and the enemy shall never dare again to attack you on such a large scale. Even if he does so, his courage and stamina will be weakened. If you are defeated, the Sabra (Arab territory) will be on your back, you can return to your area, ignoring the settlement of population there. And because you will be more conversant with the life of the land there, you shall be in a better position to launch a fresh attack on the enemy by turning against him from the Sabra and Allah will grant you victory."

(*Tabari, Vol. IV. p. 89*).

The following is added in *Iktifa.*

"It is incumbent that you should encamp in an open field, full of resources. When you encamp at a particular place, do not leave it because that will indicate weakness on your part and your enemy will feel courageous. Send spies in the enemy's forces and be on the look-out for a sudden attack. Donot rely on any one and keep me informed wherever you encamp, telling me the distance of the enemy's fore-runner and the rear guard portion of the army, indicating the climate of the place where the enemy intends to proceed. I have been intuitionally informed that you will conquer Iran and be victorious."

(*Al-iktifa, p. 376*).

(97)

TO HADRAT SA'D BIN ABI WAQQAS (R.A.A.)

Marching from Sharaf Hadrat Sa'd (R.A.A.) encamped at the station known as Mughisa, a small village, near about forty miles south east from Qaadsiyah, whereby Hadrat Sa'd despatched a few contingents to find out a proper place for encampment near Qaadsiyah, who reached 'Uzaib, a small village in north, full of grassy land of pastures and date gardens. Uzaib lay a few miles south of Qaadsiyah. The elders of the contingents in command wrote to Hadrat Sa'd (R.A.A.) that they have found out a proper place for encamping the Islamic forces, so that he (Sa'd R.A.A.) may join them with the full force of Islam. He started and encamped in an open plain between Qadsiyah and 'Uzaib, where the famous battle of Qaadsiyah was fought a few months later which shook the foundations of the Saasaanid Empire. It was a vast plain whose frontiers reached the fertile land of Iraq on one side and the Arabian Desert on the other. The clay of the plain was hard and stony, there was neither agriculture nor trees — Of course there were several pools and rivulets on the east and a few miles off in the south lay the famous oasis of 'Uzaib. The Saassanid rulers had, built military posts all along the border to keep themselves safe from the Arab onslaught. Several weeks passed by and there was no military encounter worth the name except a few border skrimishes, so Hadrat Sa'd (R.A.A.) wrote to the Caliph, Hadrat 'Umar Farooq (R.A.A.) that the army of the enemy had not yet come to fight with us. Pray to Almighty Allah for our victory. A vast country like Iraq stretches before us where it is not possible to cross except through the stream of blood. Almighty Allah has already warned us that we will be called to fight a tough and sturdy people. The following is the reply from the Caliph, Hadrat 'Umar Farooq (R.A.A.):

"Let it be known to you that as long as Hadrat Abu Bakr Siddiq (R.A.A.) remained alive, he was on the right path by the Grace of Allah. So long as he was alive, Almighty Allah showered His blessings upon him (R.A.A.) and helped him. Almighty Allah was pleased with him (R.A.A.) at time of his departure from this world. Thereafter I was put to test by entrusting the reins of Government into my hands. The discharge of this onerous duty is only possible as long as Almighty Allah's Merciful dispostion and bounty is with me. I know that the Iranian forces are ready to march upon you along with their multi-variant equipment of warfare, brave soldiers and heroes. You should not enter into any sort of discussion with them. As stated by you Qaadsiyah is replete with the necessaries of life. The expedition entrusted to you should be discharged with responsibility and due seriousness. Write to me the number of force of the Iranian army that has come to fight with you. Who is their Commander-in-Chief?

What is the distance between their king and front ranks of the forces of Iran. Do write to me candidly about the aforesaid. Glory be to Allah ! You are on an expedition whose sole care-taker is Allah, the Supreme. Allah helps those who help Him (His Deen), Who has taken upon Himself the responsibility of the success of the Muslims. He (Allah) is not the One who will turn away from His promise or responsibility. Surely He will cause Islam to prevail. If Allah wants to do good to someone, He makes them trustworthy and grateful in obedience to realize their rights and duties. Whoso is endowed with the above qualities, Allah helps them in their resolute determination of *Jehad* and fulfils their best desires and wishes. Surely, without doubt, all blessings of Allah remain in favour of the one who is free from all blemishes in the matter of his *deen* and faith. No doubt, Allah strengthens his determination of *Jehad* who is full of zeal and love of obedience. There is not the least shadow of scepticism that the station of a person is determined in the sight of Allah according to his resoluteness in determination for *Jehad*. So remember Allah much and act according to His Will. By so doing the seeker of comfort shall receive solace and success whose reward will be given in the hereafter. Your safety and success are dear to me, because you are encountering the formidable enemy of Islam, I am also a little worried on your account. So I for myself and for yourselves pray Allah for firm faith and sincere action. (*Iktifa p. 78*)

Another version of the letter under reference is to be found in (*Tabari , Vol. IV p. 89-90*).

"Do not allow fear and morbid apprehension to enter your hearts. Call upon the army personnel to secure goodness and felicity of the hereafter through keen desire of Jehad. Instil the passion for Jehad into the hearts of those who are yet devoid of it. The hardships of warfare in Jehad are a good teacher in patience and display of courage, because it is established that Allah helps one according to the intensity in his intention and thus rewards according to the magnitude of the passion for good. Let there be least injustice committed on your subordinates. All of you should pray Allah for safety and often rehearsal — there is no power to escape from evil nor to do any good except from Allah. Write to me where is the Iranian army according to your information and what is the name of their Commander-in-Chief ? I wish to provide some guidelines for you but I cannot do it because of the lack of information of your encampment and the knowledge of the condition and circumstance of the enemy. Write to me the place where the Muslims are encamping and tell me the lie of the land between you and Madaain (the Capital of Iran). This should be so clear and explicit as if I am seeing them myself. Do inform me exactly and fear Allah. Continuously and fervently pray to God and hope for success. Do not feel sanguine of victory due to your preparation and military might. Do remember that Almighty Allah has undertaken upon Himself the responsibility of your success and promised it. He is One Who never betrays His promise. There should be nothing that can deprive you from your promised success and render another nation eligible for Divine blessings.

(98)

TO HADRAT SA'D BIN ABI WAQQAS (R.A.A.)

Hadrat Sa'd (R.A.A.) after receiving the letter of the Caliph in Islam gave the geography of the surroundings of Qaadsiyah and further stated that the chiefs of the villages of Iraq who had covenanted with Khalid bin Walid (R.A.A.) and Hadrat Musanna bin Harisa (R.A.A.) had turned rebellious and are coming along with the Iranians to fight, that the command of the Iranian forces is under Rustam and other distinguished military officers. So Hadrat 'Umar Farooq (R.A.A.) gave the following reply.

"Your letter has been received and thus came to know its contents. Stay on wherever you are till the enemy attacks you. Be it remembered by you that there will be other battles after the impending one. If by the Grace of Allah the enemy is repulsed, chase him by entering his capital — Madaain. God Willing ! Madaain shall be annihilated."

(*Tabari, Vol. IV, p. 90*).

(99)

Hadrat Sa'd (R.A.A.) came to know through the informers that the Iranian forces had started from Madain and reached the out skirts of Qaadsiyah. He further informed the Centre through a report that a huge Iranian army under Rustam has come to fight along with elephants, who is not more than fifteen miles from us, and the distance between Yazdgard who is staying in the White Palace of Madain and his forces is ninety miles. Hadrat 'Umar Farooq (R.A.A.) wrote:

"Your letter was received here and thus came to know about the distance between you and Ibn-e-Kisra and the whereabouts of the enemy. Whoso is in search of Divine guidance, Almighty Allah opens his heart for Islam — the Straight Path in life. A deputation should be sent to Ibn-e-Kisra, who should invite him to Islam, Jiziyah or Warfare. If he accepts Islam, his rights and duties will be identical with you. If he does not accept Islam and agrees to pay Jiziyah, his good action shall be rewarded and his bad actions shall fall upon him. He will be granted protection to life. His dominions shall remain intact and no further action shall be carried out against him in an unjustified manner. If he refuses to accept Islam or pay Jiziyah, neither you should be afriad to fight against him nor fear his formidable force. Seek the help of Allah and have confidence in Him for victory. When you are encountering the enemy, send the brave amongst you forward, but neither in a manner derogatory to them nor in such a fashion as to endanger their lives unnecessarily. Bear with patience and fortitude the hardships of battlefield as forbearance is the key to victory. If you are victorious in the battle, chase the polytheist forces from behind, putting to sword the able-bodied young man, but leaving aside their children and women. Never allow to leave anyone who is enemy in the rear of the army. If the Iranians sue for peace, accept the same on condition that they will agree to their exile, leaving their home and hearth. The disabled and the unharmful persons can be an exception to the above. Take full heed to my instructions and act accordingly."

(*Iktifa* , *p. 279*).

(100)

TO HADRAT SA'D BIN ABI WAQQAS (R.A.A.)

"Never allow yourselves to be grieved by the large number of Iranian forces including their pomp and show in men and material. Invoke the help of Almighty Allah and keep your eyes fixed on His Grace and Benevolence. Send a deputation to Rustam comprising the brave-hearted, good-looking and prudent persons to invite him to Islam. I am sure that his firmness will be weakened by such an invitation to Islam and they will be defeated. Inform me daily about the happenings on your side."

(*Tabari, Vol. IV, p. 92*)

(101)

TO HADRAT SA'D BIN ABI WAQQAS (R.A.A.)

The above noted letter has been narrated in the following words, by *Iktifa*.

"You have sought succour from me, although an army of ten thousand is already with you, comprising such war veterans, hereoes and outstanding personalities like Malik bin 'Auf, Talha bin Rabiah, Talha bin Khuwalid and 'Umar bin Ma'di Karb (R.A.A.) and their like who are equally brave, possessing the art of warfare and horsemanship, and above all, equally devoted to the cause of Jehad so dear to them. Have trust in Almighty Allah, seek His help and victory from Him, fight with the enemy without fear, with keen devotion to love for Jehad, resolute determination, keenness to attain good, unallured by the mundane world and with justice.

Demonstrate complete forbearance during the difficult times of warfare; face the enemy with devotion; patience is the key to victory. God rewards according to the degree of passion of sacrifice one entertains. Be careful in the matter of security of the Muslims and be cautious regarding enemy's attack at night. The words that 'There is none possessing power to prevent from evil and guide to good except Allah', should be on your lips. The *Ghazis* who are apt in warfare be asked to fight the enemy. The brave should be given larger share than the due. The Muslim who kills the enemy should be given the weapons and clothes of the slain. Exemplary punishment should be awarded to the culprits. The army should be divided into seven divisions each under a military officer. I have written to Mughirah bin Shu'ba (R.A.A.) and aksed him to join you along with his army in Basra, further instructed Abu 'Ubaidah (R.A.A.) to send an army to you from Syria. Wage war with the enemy after getting the above mentioned help. Before this, if you find an opportunity to inflict a blow on the enemy, do avail of it and do not be afraid of the majority of the forces of the opponent. Often, Almighty Allah grants victory to less numbers and raises His Helping Hand off the majority in number. Tulaiha bin Khuwalid (R.A.A.), 'Umar bin Ma'di'Karb, Hanzala bin Rabia, Aus bin Madaan and Ibn-Zaidul-Khail happen to be with you. Do not appoint any one of them an officer over more than a hundred soldiers. Do consult 'Umar and Tulaiha (R.A.A.) in matters of warfare but they should not be given any military rank."

(*Iktifa , p. 281 as Quoted by Madaini*)

(102)

TO HADRAT SA'D BIN ABI WAQQAS (R.A.A.)

Do seek advice in military matters concerning warfare from Tulaiha bin Khuwalid (R.A.A.) and 'Umar bin Ma'di Karb (R.A.A.) because every craftsman knows his job but do not entrust any office to them.

(*Ibn-Abil-Hadid, Vol. III, p. 98, Izaalatul-Khifa Vol. II p. 193*).

(103)

TO HADRAT SA'D BIN ABI WAQQAS (R.A.A.)

"Refrain the *ghazis* (Heroes of Jihad in Islam) to listen to the anecdotes of the *Jahiliyah* period because by doing so the old enemities shall be revived and fresh base for ill-will and malice shall find place. As long as they wish, they should recite the Verses from the Quraan and thus receive guidance and admonition."

(*Buladhuri, Al-Ansaab , Vol. 9, p. 596*)

(104)

TO HADRAT SA'D BIN ABI WAQQAS (R.A.A.)

"Whatever military succour reaches you before the decomposition or the disposal of the corpses of the dead, you should share the booty."

(*Sarakhsi, Vol. II p. 252*).

(105)

TO HADRAT SA'D BIN ABI WAQQAS (R.A.A.)

"I have been intuitionally informed that the enemy shall be defeated in the battle against you. So eliminate doubt and scepticism from your heart and replace the same with the fear of Allah. If a military officer of your army makes a gesture to an Iranian, even in jest and humour, or makes a hint indicating safety and protection either by sign or word that may be taken for protection, do establish safety on that basis. Refrain from laughing in the battlefield. Fulfil your promise made with the enemy. Faithfulness and fidelity shows good results even at the time of faithlessness, but, if treachery is committed even by mistake, it results in ruin always. Infidelity will decrease your power, the strength of the enemy shall increase. Your success shall be converted into defeat and enemy's defeat into victory. I do warn you to avoid everything that may be indecent for the Muslims or may endanger their strength and power."

(*Tabari, Vol. IV, p. 90*)

(106)

TO HADRAT SA'D BIN ABI WAQQAS (R.A.A.)

I do hereby advise you and your army to fear Allah under all conditions, because fear of Allah is the best weapon in the face of the enemy and the most effective planning during warfare. Further your military should be cautious against their opponent but at the same time abstain from sin in a far more degree, because the enemy cannot inflict more harm than our own sins. The secret of the success of the Muslims is that their enemy is encircled within the cobweb of their sins. If it is not so, we cannot attain the upper hand over the enemy, because we are less in number and equipment.

If we are equal to the enemy in the commission of sins, the enemy will dominate us because he is greater in strength. If we are unable to succeed against the enemy on account of our good actions and disposition, certainly we cannot get the upper hand due to our military strength. Remember that Allah has appointed angels over your actions and conduct; be ashamed of them by shunning sins. Never say that the enemy is bad in comparison to us, so he will never be able to get victory over us, because sometimes it so happens that an inferior nation dominates over the superior as happened with the Magies against the Israelis because they (Israel) had incurred the displeasure of Allah on account of their misdeeds and commission of sins. God's Word came out too true as they entered the cities of the (Israelis). Pray to Almighty Allah to avoid sin as you invoke His Help and pray for victory against the opponent. I do pray for you and for myself in the same strain. Treat kindly the army during the course of marching, do not make them march excessively as they may be tired out. Do not refrain them from staying on to a place of comfort and safety, so that when they happen to meet the enemy, they should feel fresh. They are to fight against an enemy who is in his place, whose soldiers and animals are fresh. During the march of the army stay on for a day and a night so that the fatigue of the army may be done away with and may be in a position to set their weapons and other necessaries of life aright. The persons with whom you entered into a covenant and they have come under your protection, no one should be allowed to enter their settlements save those in whom you could confide that they are honest people, will not exact anything from them as you have undertaken to be their custodian. Encamp far away from their abode or settlements.

You are to fulfil your responsibility which is a test for you to be adhered to as it is a covenant and agreement on the part of the Zimmis to be complied with. Treat them fairly as long as they undertake to discharge their liability of the part of the agreement. Do not try to obtain victory over the enemy through committing excesses on the Zimmis. Spread out spies throughout the area of the enemy as and when you reach their territory and keep yourselves informed of the activities of the opponent. You should depute such Arab locals whose honesty and integrity can be trusted upon, because the report of an habitual false reporter will do no good to you. Thus the cheat or the fraudulent person will conduct secret information against you. Spread out the contingents of your forces throughout the land in between you and your enemy, intercepting the necessaries of life reaching the enemy and discovering the secrets of the enemy. Brave and prudent persons of consultation should be deputed to the contingents to gain the desired end. They should be provided with horses, be men with the passion to wage Jehad against the enemy, who could withstand under the shadow of the swords of the enemy. Personal likes and dislikes should, in no way, find place in the selection for men of contingents meant for the above stipulated purpose, as by doing so your integrity shall also be questioned and the expedition may be endangered. Thus the loss shall be far greater than the insignificant benefit of concession to the dear and near ones. The contingents should not be despatched to a place where there is apprehension to their safety and possibility of their defeat. When the enemy comes before you, recall all your contingents and muster up your full force to meet him with due planning and tactics. Do not attack unless the enemy begins his attack. Do not make haste in attacking him so that you may know his weakness and better dress yourselves, thus be conversant with the lie of the land like the locals of the area. This can be done through circumspection. By arming yourselves with such information, you will be in a position to fight against the enemy like him as he knows the whereabouts of the locality. This can be obtained through insight, Post guards on your army and be cautious about the possibility of night attack on the part of the enemy. If a captive comes to you who has not been granted protection, chop off his head to instil fear into the heart of the enemy. Allah the Supreme, is to look after you and your men — He is alone responsible for your victory and He alone is worthy from Whom Succour and Help could be sought for."

(*Ibn Abd Rabbah, Vol. I P. 67-68; Nuvairi-Nihaya-tul Arab — Egypt, Vol. 6, pp. 168-169*).

(107)

TO HADRAT SA'D BIN ABI WAQQAS (R.A.A.)

According to reports, Hadrat 'Umar Farooq (R.A.A.) had ordered Hadrat Abu 'Ubaidah (R.A.A.) that an army under the command of Yamani leader, Qais bin Makshuh Muraadi be despatched in aid of Hadrat Sa'd (R.A.A). At the time of arrival of Qais bin Makshuh at Qaadsiyah along with his seven hundred companions, the war had ended. In spite of this, the booty was demanded. So Hadrat Sa'd (R.A.A.) had to refer the matter to Hadrat 'Umar Farooq (R.A.A.) who replied as under :

"If Qais (bin Makshuh) had arrived before the burial of the slain, share in the booty may be given to them."

(*Buladuri, p. 257*)

There is another version of the letter purporting to the same contents and meanings :

In the name of Allah, Most Compassionate and Merciful. Peace be upon you. I am grateful to the sole object of Worship, Allah, except Whom there is none worthy of worship and send blessings upon His Prophet — Messenger-Muhammad (S.A.W.). I am in receipt of your letter. I am specially grateful to Almighty Allah, Who bestowed this victory through your hands. Allah has put me to test by appointing me as your chief and you are also under trial as you are under me. When the ruler is considerate and sympathetic and the subject is also well-wisher, it is the duty of the ruler to treat the subject nicely and the people should be well-disposed and the well-wisher, and grateful of the ruler. Booty is the right of those who actually participate in the battle and those who come three days later after the ensuing battle ended, they should also get something from the booty as their share. Your slaves participating in the warfare and freed within three days are entitled to the share in the booty. The *Zimmis* of the conquered land should be treated nicely.

(*Futu-hush-sham, Egypt Vol. II, p. 115*).

(108)

TO HADRAT SA'D BIN ABI WAQQAS (R.A.A.)

After the battle of Qaadsiyah say in 14, 15 or 16 A.H. Hadrat 'Umar Farooq (R.A.A.) wrote to Hadrat Sa'd bin Abi Waqqas (R.A.A.)

' Tell me about the excellence of the Standard of the *ghazis* displayed during the battle. Whether the Arab tribes fought in the same level or tried to surpass one another.

(*Iktifa, p. 282*).

(109)

TO HADRAT SA'D BIN ABI WAQQAS (R.A.A.)

Hadrat Zubrah bin Huwaijah Jashami was a young commander in the army of Hadrat Sa'd (R.A.A.). In archery and swordmanship he enjoyed extraordinary excellence. Many Iranians were killed at his hands during the battle of Qaadsiyah — among them was one Jaalinus — a great military officer. Hadrat Zubrah put off his uniform and weapons. The uniform was decorated with extreme precious embriodery so much so that its value could be calculated as seventy thousand dirhams. Hadrat Zubrah appeared before Hadrat Sa'd bin Abi Waqqas (R.A.A.) in the above uniform alongwith the weapons. Sa'd (R.A.A.) asked him to put off the uniform and the weapons and harshly reprimanded him for not waiting the orders of the Supreme Commander. Hadrat Zubrah felt excessively this extraordinary harshness and undue strictness on the part of Hadrat Sa'd (R.A.A.) and complained to the Caliph in Islam — Hadrat 'Umar Farooq (R.A.A.). Hadrat Sa'd (R.A.A.) also reported his so-called misconduct in detail. The following letter was received from Hadrat Umar Farooq (R.A.A.).

"You inflict heart-felt pain upon Zubrah — the brave, who jumped into the fire of battle fearlessly and this fire is not yet extinguished and you try to make him nervous and give pain by insulting him. Return the uniform and the weapons obtained by him after killing Jalinus and pay him five hundred dirhams more than the other *mujahideen* of the battle of Qaadsiyah, for his extraordinary performance of valour and bravery."

(*Tabari, Vol. IV, P. 135; Ibn-e-Khaldun, History of Egypt, Vol. II, p. 99*).

(110)

TO HADRAT SA'D BIN ABI WAQQAS (R.A.A.)

• Some one complained that Hadrat Zubrah (R.A.A.) stole the stemmed armlets of Jalinus that he used to put on as a mark of distinction of the army. So Hadrat Sa'd (R.A.A.) informed the Caliph, Hadrat 'Umar Farooq (R.A.A.) regarding it. The following was received as reply: "I know Hadrat Zubrah (R.A.A.) better than you. Surely he is not of that type who could hide a portion of the uniform or weapons of the slain. If your informer is a liar, may God also make him put on one pair of armlets on his arms as in the case of Hadrat Zubrah (R.A.A.). This is my instruction that whenever a *ghazi* kills an enemy in the battlefield, his weapons and uniform should be given to that *ghazi* who killed him."

(*Tabari, Vol. II, p. 99*).

(111)

TO HADRAT SA'D BIN ABI WAQQAS (R.A.A.)

"Send an army under Nadhla bin Muawiyah Ansari on the suburbs of Hulwan to carry on raids there."

(*Izaalatul Khifa, Vol. II, p. 167*).

Hulwan was the last town of the northern portions of Iraq from where began the Iranian territory.

(112)

TO HADRAT SA'D BIN ABI WAQQAS (R.A.A.)

Hadrat Sa'd (R.A.A.) despatched three hundred horsemen under Nadhlah bin Muawiyah, who carried on successful incursions in the vicinity of Hulwan and thus secured large booty. Hadrat Sa'd informed the Caliph in Islam regarding the successful expedition, so the following reply from Hadrat 'Umar Farooq (R.A.A.) was received :

' Encamp on the Mount of Hulwan along with your *Mahajir*, and Ansar *army and say my compliments to him.*"

(*Izaala-tul-Khifa Vol. II, p. 167*).

"Kanzul-'Ummal odds the following:
Because the Prophet of Allah, Muhammad (S.A.W) had informed us that one of the Wasi (one whom a will is entrusted) of. Hadrat Esa bin Maryam (S.A.) is staying in the mountain referred to above."

(113)

TO HADRAT SA'D BIN ABI WAQQAS (R.A.A.)

In the battle of Jisr the Muslims had to suffer heavy casualties resulting in the loss of manpower and prestige also. Hadrat Musanna bin Harisa had only three thousand soldiers to face the formidable foe, so he had to ask for help from the central authority at Madina. At this time the tribesmen of Bajaila of Yemen had waited upon Hadrat 'Umar Farooq (R.A.A.) in Madina, who naturally persuaded them to go to Iraq but they were hesitate to proceed to Iraqi front. On the contrary, they desired to go to Syria. Realizing the gravity of the situation Hadrat 'Umar (R.A.A.) asked them to proceed to Iraq to help Hadrat Musanna bin Harisa (R.A.A.) on condition that one fourth of the fifth of the spoils of war (booty) shall be given to them. They agreed and participated in the battle of Buwaib, that ensued and resulted in the successful end of the expedition in favour of the Muslims. Naturally one fourth of the state's share of booty was given to them according to promise. They claimed the same after the Battle of Qaadsiyah also as Jareer and his tribesmen participated in the battle. Obviously, Hadrat Sa'd bin Abi Waqqas (R.A.A.) had to refer the matter to the centre. The following was the reply :

"Now if I give one fourth of the Khums (fifth) of the booty to the people of Bajaila this will certainly tantamount to my going astray. I had promised to give one fourth on the occasion of the Battle of Buwaib to help Hadrat Musanna (R.A.A.) which they have already received. After this, they did not participate in other battles alongwith Hadrat Musanna and returned to Arab area. Reprimand them on my behalf for this unusual demand and ask them to realize the full implications of their demand on the day of Accountability as I am only the distributor to be questioned duly about my distribution.'

(*Iktifaa , p. 399*)

(114)

TO HADRAT SA'D BIN ABI WAQQAS (R.A.A.)

"Received your letter. You have stated that the Muslims are demanding the land that has been conquered by them through their sword. On receipt of my letter, see what paraphernalia of the enemy along with animals, the Muslims have brought in your camp. Distribute the same, after deducting one fifth (Khums) as state share. Leave aside the land on the rivers and canals to the peasants so that the revenue thus realized will be paid as salary of the *ghazis.* If we distribute the land thus obtained, there will remain nothing for the maintenance of the *ghazis.*"

(*Ibn-'Asakir, Vol. I, 181*)

There are slight variations in the contents and meanings of the letter under reference in *Kitabul Kharaj* by *Qazi Abu Yusuf* and the manuscript by *Yahya bin Adam Qarshi* which reads as under :

"When the Muslims pay *Zakaat* and the *Zimmi* discharges his responsibility by paying due *Jiziyah*, they should not be asked to pay one-tenth of the commercial tax which is intended for those Arab traders who enter our territory after obtaining permission to carry on trade and commerce in the land."

(115)

TO HADRAT SA'D BIN ABI WAQQAS (R.A.A.)

"Remember that Almighty Allah, the Supreme, has given you discretion of give and take due to the special nature of a particular case, but justice and rememberance of Allah is exempted from it. In the case of discharge and dispensation of justice, it is incumbent to do justice — a fact that seems to be very light but possèsses great power as it is a potential to eradicate cruelty. *Kufr* (Disobedience to Allah) is responsible for all injustices and inequities. The Zimmis in Iraq, who stuck to their covenants and also did not help the enemy, their agreements should be kept restored and

Jiziyah be realized from them. The Iranians who claim that they were forced to break their promise and fight against the Muslims, but neither they fought against you nor left their home and hearth, it is left to you to accept their plea or exile them."

(*Tabari, Vol. IV, p. 145*)

(116)

TO THE MILITARY COMMANDERS IN IRAQ

"The non-zimmi landlords, who remained in their respective areas, should be treated like *Zimmis*, as they did not leave their home and hearth and also they did not fight against you. The farmers also who showed the above mentioned conduct they should also be treated accordingly. The Iranians who claim that they did not engage into battle against you and can substantiate their plea on solid proof, they should be treated also as Zimmis and whosoever is unable to support and prove his stand, his claim should be rejected. The land holders who rendered help to the enemy, left their homes and hearth, it is left to your option to make them Zimmis after returning their property in land and other articles. If they do not wish to return, their lands and property may be distributed among yourselves."

(*Tabari, Vol. IV, P. 145*)

(117)

TO HADRAT SA'D BIN ABI WAQQAS (R.A.A.)

Hadrat Sa'd (R.A.A.) wrote to the Caliph in Islam to seek permission to distribute a plot of land among the Muslim military officers that fell into their hands without fighting. The Caliph wrote back as under :

"If you wish, you may distribute among yourselves the said plot of land or you may leave it to the land holders to till the same, so that the coming generations may be benefitted by its income. Further, it is my apprehension if you divide it among yourselves there will arise conflict on account of its watering through irrigation etc., and thus you will start killing each other amongst yourselves."

(*Al-Istikhrajul-Ahkamul-Kharaj*, *Abdur Rehman*, *Hanbali*, *Egypt*, *1924*, *p. 14*).

(118)

TO HADRAT SA'D BIN ABI WAQQAS (R.A.A.)

Hadrat 'Umar Farooq (R.A.A.) ordered the seige of Madaain two months after the conquest of Qaadsiyah. The Iranians offered resistence on their way to Madaain but every time they were repulsed. Madaain was a collection of several cities and palaces, mostly situated on the eastern bank of Tigris, its adjacent town, Behr Sair was connected through a bridge with a strong fortress inside and situated on the eastern bank of Tigris, its adjacent town, Behr Sair was connected through a bridge with a strong fortress inside and situated on the Western bank. The Iranians had dug a trench to check the onslaught of the Muslims. The Muslim seige continued for two months, meanwhile, the contingents of Hadrat Sa'd bin Abi Waqqas (R.A.A.) continued their forays on the settlements that lay in the mid of the Tigris and the Euphārates, they captured about 100000 farmers and wrote to Hadrat 'Umar Farooq (R.A.A.), regarding the disposal and treatment to be meted out to these captured peasants. The following is the reply :

"The peasants that have been brought before you may be awarded protection provided they remained in their houses and did not render help to the Iranians against you. Those of them as such may be provided protection even if they did not come to you. *Iktifa* adds adds: "And those who left their homes and hearths and fell in your hands, you are at liberty to deal with them."

(*Tabarani, Vol. IV p. 168*).

(119)

TO HADRAT SA'D BIN ABI WAQQAS (R.A.A.)

On receipt of the news of conquest of Madaain, Hadrat 'Umar Farooq (R.A.A.) wrote the following : "I enjoin upon you to fear Allah because of this fear of God one becomes fortunate and without this one renders himself liable to be unfortunate. You know very well the bounties that have been bestowed upon us by Allah. He saved us from polytheism and the polytheists, granted salvation and freedom from paying respect to their idols and thus showed us the straight way of guidance from the deluded one. And we came out of the clutches of the Quraish polytheists in such a condition that several Muslims were on the back of a camel along with their travelling kit, only with one blanket, that was put on by us with their respective turns. Those of us who reached Madina, they were tried to the core and the rest who remained at Mecca, were subjected to different kinds of tortures while their dearest and nearest ones were on the fore-front. (Under these conditions) the Messenger of Allah, Muhammad (S.A.W) used to say on solemn affirmation:

> The treasure-stores of the Qaiser and the Kisra will fall under your hands.'

Whoso heard this was wonder struck. God kept you alive to fulfil the prophecy of the Prophet (S.A.W.) at your hands. Do not entangle yourselves under the paraphernalia of the worldly riches till you go to meet those *mujahids* who discarded this mundane world and passed away in tattered clothes, whose stomachs were sticking to their backs and there was no check between them and Lord-Allah: The world failed to enchant them and they could not be deluded by the worldly riches. Make such persons as your guide and do not be led away by the love of worldly glories, pomp and show. Remain to be praise worthy and the blessed nature whom Almighty Allah praises thus:

> We made them the guide, they guide the people to the right path, We made them to do good, offer prayers, pay Zakat and they are the obedient to Us." (21:73)

(*Al-Iktifa, p: 407*)

(120)

TO HADRAT QUTBAH BIN QATADAH SUDUSI (R.A.A.)

In 12 A.H., Qutbah, an Arab leader was leading forays on the Iranian villages and military check-posts in the delta of Tigris and Euphrates. In the same year Hadrat Abu Bakr Siddiq (R.A.A.) ordered Hadrat Khalid bin Walid (R.A.A.), who was staying in Yamama after having done away with Muslaimah, the impostor, to proceed to the help of Musanna bin Harisa (R.A.A.) who was leading forays in the vicinity of Heerah, particularly the villages and the military check posts. On the way, Hadrat Khalid bin Walid (R.A.A.) caputured Haribah, an important check post. This was done with the assisstance of Qutbah, who further carried on military forays, subjugating the Iranian landholders to pay *Jiziyah.*, Khalid bin Walid (R.A.A.) left for Heerah, after entrusting the Arab frontiers to Qutbah, who was of the opinion that the Iranian landholders could be subjugated easily and he will be able to exile them from Shat-tul-Arab. He wrote to Hadrat 'Umar Farooq (R.A.A.) to send him a small force in support of the intended expedition. 'Umar Farooq (R.A.A.) wrote back the following :

"I am in receipt of your letter. You have made a mention in the letter regarding the successful forays carried on by you. This practice is quite praiseworthy and proper. Till receipt of further instructions from me, you remain firmly established where you are Be careful about the enemy, so that he may not be in a position to harm your companions."

(121)

TO HADRAT 'UTBAH BIN GHAZWAAN (R.A.A.)

In 14 A.H. Hadrat 'Umar Farooq (R.A.A.) despatched a contingent of 500 strong in aid of Qutbah (R.A.A.) under the command of Utbah bin Ghazwaan (R.A.A.).

It was at this time that the famous international port of Ubulla was captured. This was considered to be an astounding victory. One Muslim, named Salma, received a cooking pot as a booty that was considered to be of brass but it was of real gold. When it came to the knowledge of Hadrat 'Utbah, he asked Salma to return the cooking pot, who refused to do so. The matter was referred to Hadrat'Umar Farooq (R.A.A.) for necessary guidance, who gave the reply as under:

" Oath should be administered to Salma on the fact at the time of receiving the cooking pot, he thought it to be of brass. If he does not, the cooking pot should be seized forcibly from him for distribution among the Muslims."

(*Tabari, Vol. IV. p. 152*)

(122)

TO HADRAT 'UTBAH BIN GHAZWAAN (R.A.A.)

Hadrat 'Utbah (R.A.A.) encamped in Khareebah, a place near whieh Basra was inhabited and requested Hadrat 'Umar Farooq (R.A.A.) to grant permission for the establishment of a permanant cantonment. So the Caliph in Islam replied as under:

"Gather all your forces at a place where should be water and pastures in abundance, and inform me about its Iocation and geography."

(*Buladhuri, p. 341*)

(123)

TO HADRAT 'UTBAH BIN GHAZWAAN (R.A.A.)

"Be it clear that now you are the chief among your companions there. Your words are effective and your orders are implemented. It would be a real calamity if you act in a way that may not increase your status in the eyes of the people and Allah, and you may start committing excesses upon those who are less in rank; so shun Iuxuriant way of life as you avoid calamity and trouble; eschew such mistakes that cannot be forgiven, peace and blessings,

(*Ibn Abd Rabbah, Vol. 3, p. 151*)

(124)

TO HADRAT HARQOOS BIN ZUBAIR SA'DI (R.A.A.)

"It has come to my notice that you have encamped at a high place where it is difficult to ascend, You encamp on a plain so that none of the Muslims or the Zimmis should feel difficulty in reaching you. Whatever mission is entrusted to you, be always ready in its execution. If you do so, you will be rewarded in the Hereafter and will also live a happy life in this world. Do not be hasty or negligent in the matter of discharging your duty otherwise you will lose peace and tranquility in this world and the felicity of the Hereafter."

(*Tabari, Vol. IV, p. 212*)

(125)

TO HADRAT 'UTBAH BIN GHAZWAAN (R.A.A.)

"Ask the Muslims not to commit excesses upon non-Muslim Zimmis. Be fearful of the fact that you may lose your authority or government on account of your infidelity or cruelty, and some other nation may inherit the authority on account of your misdeeds.

Government and authority has been acquired by you through the help of Allah under a convenant that you will remain true to your words and Almighty Allah has enjoined upon you to remain faithful. So it is incumbent that you should fulfil your obligatons made by you with Allah and carry out His commands. By so doing you will always be eligible for His help and assitance."

(*Tabari, Vol. IV, p. 212*)

(126)

TO HADRAT 'ALA BIN HADRAMI (R.A.A.)

Since the days of Hadrat Abu Bakr Siddiq (R.A.A.) Hadrat 'Ala (R.A.A.) was the governor of Bahrain.

"You have been appointed governor of Basra in place of Hadrat 'Utbah bin Ghazwan (R.A.A.) Remember that you are proceeding to a person who belongs to the foremost category of the *Muhajirs* whose good-ending in the Hereafter has already been promised by Almighty Allah. I have not removed Hadrat 'Utbah (R.A.A.) on the ground that honesty, strict action in the matter of truth and rare qualities of bravery are lacking in him but I am of the opinion that you will be more suited on the front of Basra. Be consderate towards the rights and rank of Hadrat 'Utbah (R.A.A.). I had appointed another person the governor of Basra who died on the way before reaching there. If Allah wills that you should be governor there, surely you will be. If Allah Wills to continue 'Utbah (R.A.A.) as governor surely he will remain so. All rights belong to Allah — the Cherisher of the entire universe — Whoso command is operative and effective upon every one including humans. You must not forget that God's Command is always invoilable. He is the Protector of His commands as He has sent it. So fix your eyes upon Him only, for Whose pleasure you have been created and your life should be spent for His sake. Do not attach your heart on anything except Allah. Surely this world is a passing phase and the Hereafter is eternal and abiding. It is not proper in any way that you should be oblivious of the Hereafter on account of worldly pleasures of hedonistic life. The blessings of the Hereafter are eternal and ever-lasting. Seek refuge of Almighty Allah from such actions that may incur the displeasure of Allah. Surely Allah grants excellence in knowledge and wisdom (Hikmat) whom He Wills. We pray Allah to save us (you and I) from His chastisement."

(*Ibn-Sa'd, Vol. IV, p. 78*)

(127)

TO HADRAT 'UTBAH BIN GHAZWAAN (R.A.A.)

Hadrat 'Ala bin Hadrami was a keen competitor of Hadrat Sa'd bin Abi Waqqas (R.A.A.). Both were possessed of the spirit of competition between them as both of them desired to excel each other in matters of achievement. When it came to the knowledge of Hadrat 'Ala (R.A.A.) that Hadrat Sa'd bin Abi Waqqas (R.A.A.) has attained an astounding victory in the battle of Qadsiyah and has shaken the very foundations of the Government of Kisra and is futher proceeding towards Iraq, he (R.A.A.) was pre-possessed by a desire to secure same formidable victory in Iran. He, without permission of the Caliph, landed his forces from Bahrain through the sea-route in the famous province of Faras in Iran. After some preliminary conquests they had to encounter enormous difficulties as the Persians took hold of thier coastal base, burnt their boats During a fight in Taaus, heavy losses were inflicted on both sides. So the striken Arab forces marched towards Basra via land route, so they were surrounded by the Persians. When the news of this sad encounter in naval warfare reached Hadrat 'Umar Farooq (R.A.A.), he was higly annoyed with Hadrat 'Ala (R.A.A.) He was deposed from the governorship of Bahrain and made him dependent of Hadrat Sa'd (R.A.A.). Side by side, the Caliph wrote back to the Governor of Basra to save Hadrat 'Ala and his forces from further discomfiture:

"Ala Hadrami (R.A.A.) proceeded with an army by the sea-route to attack the Persians, who took possession of his fleet by cutting off his way to retreat. This step was undertaken by him without my permission and, I think, the pleasure of Allah was also not before him. I apprehend that if he is not assisted at this junction, the enemy will deprive him of all by getting hold of him. So despatch a force from Basra and recall him before he is destroyed by the enemy."

(*Tabari, Vol. IV, p. 213*).

(128)

TO HADRAT 'ALA BIN HADRAMI (R.A.A.)

"Almighty Allah endowed authority on the ground that people should obey because in the absence of obedience there is disorder, lawlessness and confusion in society. You have prepared an army, attacked the Persian territory, endangering the lives of the Muslims without my permission. I have asked the governor of Basra to send an army for your help and save you from destruction. Now you are not permitted to go to Bahrain. You should proceed post haste to Sa'd bin Abi Waqqas (R.A.A.) If I knew that there is something else that is disliked by you more than the subordination of Hadrat Sa'd bin Abi Waqqas (R.A.A.), surely I would have done that."

(*Nasikh-ut-Tawarikh, Vol. IV, p. 397*)

(129)

TO HADRAT MUGHIRAH BIN SHU'BA (R.A.A.)

After the death of 'Utbah bin Ghazwaan (R.A.A.) the founder and governor of Basra, Hadrat Mughirah bin Shu'ba (R.A.A.) was appointed as the governor of Basra along with its dependencies. During the days of Hadrat 'Utbah (R.A.A.), Naafi bin Harith (R.A.A.) had started the business of breeding the horses in one of the green and fertile plains of Shat-al-Arab, near Basra. In one of the meetings with the Caliph, Hadrat Naafi (R.A.A.) requested him to grant the fertile-land on which he is breeding the horses. So 'Umar Farooq (R.A.A.) wrote the following recommendatory letter to the Governor of Basra :

"*In the name of Allah, the Compassionate the Merciful.*
Peace and Blessing of Servant of Allah 'Umar, the commander of the believers, to Mughirah bin Shu'ba (R.A.A.)

I am grateful to Almighty Allah except Whom there is

none worthy of worship. Be it known to you that 'Abdullah (Naafi') told me that he cultivated near Basra and bred the horses as well, whereas none paid any heed towards this profession. This step is prasie-worthy on his part. You help him in cultivation and breeding of horses. I have permitted him to do cultivation. Give him the land he had cultivated upon it, provided that it does not belong to the Zimmis or it is irrigated by their waters. I do further recommend good treatment for Hadrat Naafi (R.A.A.). Peace and Blessings of Allah be upon you."

(*Buladhuri, p. 356*).

There is another version of the letter in Buladhuri etc. purporting to the same meaning and contents.

(130)

TO HADRAT MUGHIRAH BIN SHU'BA (R.A.A.)

There seems to be lot of misunderstanding existing in the case of Hadrat Mughirah bin Shu'ba (R.A.A.) and a woman named Ume-Jamil belonging to a respectable family whose husband died while fighting in the battle-field. Reports had reached Hadrat 'Umar Farooq (R.A.A.) regarding the love-episode between Hadrat Mughirah (R.A.A.) and Umm-Jâmil. May be this due to misunderstanding and back-biting. Anyhow, Hadrat Mughirah (R.A.A.) was removed from the office of governor of Basra and Hadrat Abu Musa Ash'ari (R.A.A.) was appointed in his place under the following orders from Hadrat 'Umar Farooq (R.A.A.) .

"I have received a serious news. I am sending Hadrat Abu Musa Ash'ari (R.A.A.) to be governor of Basra. Hand over the charge of Governorship to him and proceed to (Madina) post haste."

(*Tabari, Vol. IV, p. 207*)

There is another version of the letter under reference purporting to the same meaning and content:

"It has come to my notice that you have committed such an abominal act that it would have been better if you had died before its commission"

(*Ibn-Sa'd Vol. 7, p. 131*)

(131)

TO THE PEOPLE OF BASRA

Hadrat 'Umar Farooq (R.A.A.) sent the following despatch to the people of Basra alongwith the above cited letter meant for Hadrat Mughirah (R.A.A.):

"I am sending Abu Musa (R.A.A.) duly appointed as governor, so that he may help the grieved persons against the tyrants, fight with the enemies with your help and assistance. Help the Zimmis, realize the revenue for distribution amongst you and keep the government roads safe and secure."

(*Tabari, Vol. IV, p. 207*)

(132)

TO HADRAT SA'D BIN ABI WAQQAS (R.A.A.)

After a stay about eight months in Madaain, the headquarter of Hadrat Sa'd bin Abi Waqqas (R.A.A.) it came to his notice thorugh the informers that an Iranian force had gathered at Jalula to fight with the Muslims. Another army, composing of the different Arab tribes and the Byzantines had been collected at Tikrit. Jalula lay about hundred miles from Madaain on the north of Iraq, near the highway known as Iraq and Khurasaan highway and Tikrit was situated on the Western Tigris in between Mosaul and Madaain. It was a fortified town. Hadrat Sa'd (R.A.A.) informed the Caliph regarding the movement of the forces of the enemy. The following two different orders were sent by the Caliph, Hadrat 'Umar Farooq (R.A.A.) :

"Send a contingent of twelve thousand army to Jalula under the command of Hashim bin 'Utbah whose front should be under the command of Qa'qa bin 'Umar, the right under the command of Hadrat Sa'd bin Maalik (R.A.A.) the left under the charge of 'Umar bin Maalik and the rear guard under the command of 'Umar bin Murrah Juhani."

(*Tabari, Vol. IV, p. 179*).

(133)

TO HADRAT SA'D BIN ABI WAQQAS (R.A.A.)

The Second firman (Order) reads as under:

"Despatch an army under Hadrat 'Abdullah bin Mut'im to face the Arab and Byzantine armies under the command of Intaaq — Its front, right, left, rear guard and the other contingents should be under the leadership of Riba'ee bin Ifkil 'Anzi, Harith bin Hassan Zahli, Furat bin Hayyan Ajili, Haani bin Qais and 'Ur-fa-ja bin Har-samah respectively."

(*Tabari, Vol. IV, p. 186*)

(134)

TO SA'D BIN ABI WAQQAS (R.A.A.)

"If by the Grace of Allah the armies of Mehran and Intaaq are defeated, the front guard leader Qa'qa bin 'Amr should be asked to create checkposts in the frontiers of Iraq and Jibaal."

(*Tabari, Vol. IV, p. 179*).

(135)

TO SA'D BIN ABI WAQQAS (R.A.A.)

"Stay, wherever you are. Do not chase the Iranians. On the other hand, prepare a cantonment and settlement place for Muslims, but there should be no river between them and myself."

(*Tabari, Vol. IV, p. 141*)

(136)

TO HADRAT SA'D BIN ABI WAQQAS (R.A.A.)

After the conquest of Jalula, the commander of the Muslim forces, Hashim bin 'Utbah, left an army guarding Jalula and returned himself to Madaain. During this time, an Iranian force entered Iraq to fight with the Muslims in th province of Jibal. The Caliph, Hadrat 'Umar Farooq (R.A.A.) was apprised of the exact local situation. So the following reply from the Centre:

"Despatch an army under the command of Hadrat Darraar bin Khattab whose leader of the front force should be Ibn-Huzail Asadi and the Commanders of the two wings be 'Abdullah bin Raasi and Mudaarib bin Fulaan Ajli."

(*Tabari, Vol. IV, p. 187*).

(137)

TO THE MUSLIM GHAZIS

The following letter was addressed to the Muslim *Ghazis* encamping in Khaniqeen, where the defeated Persian forces had gathered round, a place about twenty to twentyfive miles north east of Jalula leading to Hulwaan. An Arab Muslim force from Jalula inflicted a crushing defeat .upon them and captured the place. The following are the instructions from the Caliph, Hadrat 'Umar Farooq (R.A.A.)

"When you beseige a fort and the residents therein, sue for peace on condition that they should be treated in accordance with the Divine intention Please do not accept this plea because you do not know the implications of divine intention in this regard: but on the contrary they should be given to understand that they will be dealt with according to your discretion and sense of judgement and thereafter deal with them accordingly. Whenever any solider from your side says to a soldier of the enemy! Laa taujal or laa-takhaf or ma-taras or Laa tad-hal all purporting to mean — 'do not be afraid of' — all thse words are synomymous meaning thereby that Peace and protection have been extended to them because Almighty Allah knows all languages."

(*Abu Yousuf, Kanzul-'Ummal, Vol. 3, p. 126*).

(138)

TO HADRAT SA'D BIN ABI WAQQAS (R.A.A.)

Hadrat Sa'd bin Abi Waqqas (R.A.A.) came to know that an army from Mysopotamia had arrived in aid of Heraclius and another to fight with the Muslims in the vicinity of the Western Tigris, nearing Madaain at a place known Hait. The Centre Madina was informed of the conditions prevailing and the local situation then existing. The Caliph wrote back the following :

"The forces of the Jazirah should be made to face a Muslim army under the command of 'Amr bin Maalik bin Utbah at Hait, the herald of the army be under the command of Harith bin Zaid 'Aamri, right and left of the force under the command of Ribaie bin 'Aamir and Maalik bin Habib respectively."

(*Tabari, Vol. IV, p. 187*)

(139)

TO THE CONQUERORS OF IRAQ

The party of the elite — conquerors in Iraq requested the Caliph, Hadrat 'Umar Farooq (R.A.A.) to grant them permission to distribute Sawaafi (lands belonging to the royal family) among the army. The following reply was received:

"Out of the five shares of Sawaafi (Royal) four parts of the same may be distributed among the conqueror army of Iraq and the fifth (khums) of the same be sent to me for incurring expenses under the fixed heads. If the conquerors wish to be settled in the Sawaafi, they are entitled to it."

(*Tabari, Vol. IV. p. 187*)

As stated above, Sawaafi meant:

(1) The land of the royal family
(2) Whose income was spent upon the construction of highways, postal routes, repair of bridges, and the places of fire worship,
(3) Whose masters had run away or killed in the battlefield.
(4) Where there were forests and
(5) Where there were tanks, pools and springs.

Sawaafi yielded an income from twenty to thirty-five lacs of Rupees according to the rate of Rupee prevailing at that time.

In another letter of similar description, content and meaning, Hadrat 'Umar Farooq (R.A.A.) absolved himself of all responsibility if the conquerors do not take possession of the conquered land called 'Fay' which under the present context means state land belonging to the royal family.

(140)

TO HADRAT SA'D BIN ABI WAQQAS (R.A.A.)

The Commander-in-Chief of the Muslim forces in Iran, Hadrat Sa'd bin Abi Waqqas (R.A.A). ordered the survey of the peasants from Madaain to Jalula, numbering more than one lakh and thirty thousand, and asked for the disposal of these farmers from the Caliph Hadrat 'Umar Farooq (R.A.A.) The following reply was received:

"Leave aside the peasantry for cultivation: among those who fought against you or ran away with the enemy and have been captured by you, they should be meted out the same treatment as given to other farmers in Iraq. Whenever I issue instructions for a people of particular profession, they are equally applicable to similar persons in profession."

(*Tabari, Vol. IV, p. 184*)

(141)

TO HADRAT SA'D BIN ABI WAQQAS (R.A.A.)

The above letter dealt with the treatment to be shown to farmers, while Sa'd bin Abi Waqqas (R.A.A.) sought guidance from the Caliph regarding non-professionalists so the following reply came in :

"You are at liberty to deal with the non-professionals, provided they have not been distributed amongst yourselves. Those among them who fought with you and left their homes, hearth and properties, all these belong to the Muslims. If you have invited them to come back and they consented to pay Jiziya and their property had been returned to them before distribution, they will enjoy the status of Zimmis. If you have not invited them to come back, the Muslim conquerors will be the owners of their estates as *Ghaazis.*"

(*Tabari, Vol. IV, p. 184*)

(142)

After the complete subjugation of Iraq, a deputation from Madaain waited upon the Caliph at Madina. Hadrat 'Umar Farooq (R.A.A.) saw the lean and thin faces of these persons and enquired the reason for it. They replied that the climate of the region did not suit them. 'Umar Farooq (R.A.A.) referred the matter to Hadrat Sa'd bin Abi Waqqas (R.A.A.) who certified the statement of the deputationists.

The following *firman* (order) was issued by the Caliph:

"The Arabs can be acclimatized to the same place as is suited to their camels. Hadrat Salman (R.A.A.) and Hadrat Huzaifa (R.A.A.) be directed to find out such healthy place that is available in the vicinity of the desert and the river. But, let there be no river intercepting in between you and

myself."

(*Tabari, Vol. IV, p. 189*)

(143)

TO HADRAT SA'D BIN ABI WAQQAS (R.A.A.)

In compliance of the above firman (order) the foundation of Kufa was laid in an extrmely extensive plain in the 17 A.H., whose one side lay adjacent to the cultivated land of Tigris and the other side touched the Arabian Desert, The foundation stone of the mosque was laid in the first instance. In front of the mosque lay the offices, public treasury (Baitul-maal) and the residence of the governor.

After a few days, someone broke into the baitul-maal and a large amount was stolen. The Caliph was informed of the same, so the following despatch from the Caliph was received:

"Rebuild the mosque adjacent to the residence of the governor *(Daarul-Imaarah)* in such a way that the inner portion of the mosque should be adjacent to the governor's residence, making the treasury safe due to the constant presence of the devotees in the mosque."

(*Buladhuri, Vol. IV, p. 194*)

(144)

According to some narrators, Hadrat Sa'd bin Abi Waqqas (R.A.A.) requested for the permission to build a residence for the governor, the following reply was received.

"Build a place that may provide protection from sun and rain."

(*Izaalatul-Khifa*)

The following words are added in the Taa-rikh-e-Damishq by Ibn-e-Asaakir"

"The world is a temporary abode."

(145)

TO HADRAT SA'D BIN ABI WAQQAS (R.A.A.)

As per instruction from the Caliph, Hadrat Sa'd (R.A.A.) shifted the mosque adjacent to the governor's residence — a mud building. This may be the cause that it was broken in and a large amount of money was stolen as stated above. An Iranian chief constructed the same with lime and stone under his supervision. Stone-pillars were also erected, giving it a palatial shape with broad gateway in front of the same. There was a market round the governor's residence full of noise, creating disturbance in the performance of official duties. People of the place set the news afloat that Hadrat Sa'd (R.A.A.) had instructed the contractor to prepare the building that may be noise proof. News reached 'Umar Farooq (R.A.A.) that Hadrat Sa'd (R.A.A. had constructed a palace for his residence with a huge gate outside. This was disliked by the Caliph. So he sent his special messenger, Muhammad bin Muslimah, entrusted him the following letter with clear cut instructions to burn the gate of the palace that was immediately complied with:

"It has come to my notice that you have built a palace for your residence, known as Qasr-e-Sa'd and have erected a gate in your palace, thus creating a hinderance between yourselves and the public. This is not your palace but the palace of destruction. Reside in its portion adjacent to the *baitul-maal*, the rest of the building should be closed. Do not put any gate in between you and the people to enable them to see you, to present their petitions and grievances before you without hinderance. They should have access to you and should have the opportunity to meet you while they are out from their houses."

(*Izaalatul-Khifa*)

(146)

Hadrat 'Umar Farooq (R.A.A.) had appointed Hadrat Usman bin Hanif (R.A.A.) as Commissioner to survey and assess the revenue on land irrigated by River Tigris. When the work was completed, Hadrat 'Umar Farooq (R.A.A.) directed the following in the matter of levy of revenue:

"On every Jarib (160 Sq. yds) whether cultivated practically or not, one *dirham* in cash and one *qafeez* (measure) of corn, ten dirhams from the cultivation of grapes and from vegetables five dirhams should be levied, but dates and other fruit-yielding trees should be exempted from taxation."
(Zaili'e Vol. III, p. 400)

(147)

TO HADRAT 'USMAN BIN HANEEF (R.A.A.)

The major portion of the land and estate in Iraq belonged to the Iranian royal family. Hadrat 'Umar Farooq (R.A.A.) granted estates to deserving cases from this land. One of them was Jareer bin Abdullah Bajali, who displayed exemplary valour and devotion during the Iraq warfare and thus asked the Caliph to grant him land in Iraq. The Caliph Hadrat 'Umar Farooq (R.A.A.) sent him to 'Usman bin Haneef (R.A.A.) with the following letter:

"Grant Jareer bin 'Abdullah Bajali exactly the land that is needed by him for peaceful living, nor more no less."
(Tabari, Vol. IV, p. 148)

(148)

Usman bin Haneef (R.A.A.) did not sanction the land as he doubted the veracity of the document that was confirmed by the Caliph in the following words:

"The statement made by Jareer regarding grant of land

and the letter are genuine. Do execute the same. It is good that you have referred the matter to me."

(Tabari, Vol. IV, p. 148)

(149)

TO HADRAT HUZAIFA BIN YAMAAN (R.A.A.)

Hadrat Huzaifa bin Yamaan (R.A.A.) was appointed Commissioner for the survey of land and assessment of revenue that was watered by the Tigris. His headquarter was Madaain, the Central city in Iraq. He married a Jewish woman. The Caliph came to know of it, who wrote the following :

"It has come to my knowledge that you have married a woman of the People of Book, residing in Madaain. Divorce her."

(Tabari, Vol. I, P. 147).

There are two or three versions of the letter under reference purporting the same meaning wherein the Caliph in Islam expressed apprehension that this will set a very bad precedence for other simple Muslims, who will entertain ideas that Huzaifa (R.A.A.) had married a Kafir woman of his choice. They will also marry likewise and will be infatuated by the outward appearance and beauty of the Zimmi women, thus putting the Arab women to a very serious and difficult test to come out successful. (*Izaa-la-tul-khifa, Vol. 2, P. 181*).

There is another version based on different sources of the same letter as mentioned above.

(150)

Hadrat Huzaifa bin Yamaan (R.A.A.) protested to the Caliph in Islam, asking as to the validity of the marriage with a woman of the people of the Scriptures. The following is the reply of the Caliph :

"No doubt the marriage with a woman of the People of Book is not prohibited: since the 'ajami woman are fascinating and charming with regard to their outward beauty, they will gain dominance over the Arab women."

(*Kanzul-'Ummaal*)

(151)

Hadrat Huzaifa (R.A.A.) reported to the Khalifa that some people had embraced Islam before the levy of revenue while others became Muslim after the imposition of revenue and the jiziyah in his area. The following is the reply from the Khalifa :

"Those who accepted Islam before the levy of revenue and the Jiziyah, realize only one-tenth (ushr) from them and cancel the realization of Jiziyah from them. Those who became Muslim after the imposition of Jiziyah and revenue, realize only the revenue from such category of people because their land had come into our possession when they were non-Muslims."

(*Abdur Rahman Hambli, Al-Istikhraj-ul-Ahkam-ul-Kharaj*).

(152)

TO HUZAIFA BIN YAMAAN (R.A.A.)

Hadrat Huzaifa (R.A.A.) had informed the Caliph Hadrat 'Umar Farooq (R.A.A.) that large quantity of ration and huge amount of money is still available after distribution. So he sent the following reply :

"This wealth has been obtained by the ghaazis (Muslim conquerors) after fighting with the non-Muslims. This is neither the property of 'Umar (R.A.A.) nor his family. Do distribute the same among the *ghaazis.*".

(*Kanzul-'Ummaal, Vol. 3, p. 317*)

(153)

TO HADRAT SA'D BIN ABI WAQQAS (R.A.A.)

Hadrat Abu 'Ubaidah bin Jarrah (R.A.A.) had encamped in his headquarter, Homs, after the conquest of Syria and the expulsion of the Byzantine Emperor, Qaiser. Khalid bin Walid (R.A.A.) continued his forayes into the northern frontier towns. It was at this time that the Christians of Mesopotamia entered into a secret alliance with the Qaiser to attack the Muslims in Homs along with their concerted forces and thus they intercepted all routes leading to Homs to cut off supplies to the Muslims in men and money. Naturally, Hadrat Abu 'Ubaidah bin Jarrah (R.A.A.) beseiged himself in the fortress of Homs sent a strong, urgent letter to the Caliph, apprising him of the exact local situation and demanding military succour in this hour of need. So Hadrat 'Umar Farooq (R.A.A.) wrote the following letter to Hadrat Sa'd (R.A.A.), who had settled in Kufa by now :

"The day you receive this letter, despatch a force to Homs the same day under the command of Qa'qaa' bin 'Amr as Hadrat Abu 'Ubaidah had been beseiged there. The army should be ordered to reach Homs as expeditiously as possible."

(*Tabari , Vol. IV, p. 195*)

(154)

To HADRAT SA'D BIN ABI WAQQAS (R.A.A.)

"Send an army under the command of Hadrat Suhail bin 'Adi for Raqqa, a city of Jazirah. It is the people of Jazirah who have instigated the Byzantines to launch an attack upon Homs as has been done by the people of Qarqaisiya already. The second force should be despatched, under the command of 'Abdullah bin 'Utbaan (R.A.A.) to Nasibain, a town in Jazirah because its people were also instigated by the inhabitants of Qarqaisiya to make an assault on Muslims.

When the above two commanders finish with Riq-qah and Nasibain they should be asked to proceed to the (Capital of Jazirah) — Ru-haa. A third contingent, under Walid bin 'Uqbah; may be desptached to Jazirah for the Christians compri-ing of the Arab tribes of Rabi'ah and Tanoukh. And also send 'Ayaz bin Ghanam (R.A.A.) for the Jazirah expedition. In the battle, if ensues, all the individual commanders shall be under the command of 'Ayaz (R.A.A.)."

(*Tabari, Vol. IV, p. 196*)

(155)

TO THE QAISER, BYZANTINE

As already stated Hadrat 'Umar Farooq (R.A.A.) had entrusted the expedition of Jazirah to the four commanders, one of them was Hadrat Walid bin 'Uqbah (R.A.A.). He was under orders from the Caliph 'Umar Farooq (R.A.A.), to muster up the Arab tribes in Jazirah to be with the Muslims to fight against the Byzantines. This invitation was accepted by all the Arab tribes except the tribe of Ayaad. Some of these tribesmen accepted Islam but several thousand persons of Ayaad tribe left their Muslim Area residences and went to the Byzantine dominion. Naturally, Hadrat Walid bin 'Uqbah (R.A.A.) informed the centre, so Hadrat 'Umar Farooq (R.A.A.) wrote the following letter replete with political warning and persuasion :

"It has been brought to my notice that an Arab tribe has left our country and went to your dominion. Please return the tribe to us else we will break our covenant with the Christians of Darul-Islam, send them to your country after exiling them."

(*Tabari, Vol. IV, p. 198*)

The above letter produced the desired effect. Four thousand persons of the Ayaad tribe returned to their respective places under Muslim domination. This was under orders of the Qaiser. Jazirah was captured by the Muslims either in 17 A.H. or 19 A.H. according to the authority of *Saif bin 'Umar* and *Maqbool Ibn-Ishaque* respectively.

(156)

One of the distinguished Christian Arab tribes Taghlab, resided in Jazirah. Hadrat Walid bin 'Uqbah (R.A.A.) invited the elite of the tribe to accept Islam, but they were not inclined to relinquish their faith and insisted for protection on the basis of payment of Jiziyah. Hadrat Walid bin Uqbah (R.A.A.) put forward his own point of view that the Arabs are not entitled to pay Jiziyah, so they will have to embrace Islam. The elite of tribe again pressed their demand and further requested Hadrat Walid (R.A.A.) to send their case to the Central authority in Islam, the Caliph 'Umar Farooq (R.A.A.). The following reply was received from the Caliph in this connection :

"Only the Arab inhabitants of the Arabian Peninsula are required to accept Islam. The Arabs of *Taghlabi* tribe may be permitted to pay Jiziyah, if they do not accept Islam as they are outside the pale of Arabian Peninsula. This should be done on condition that they should promise not to force their children into Christianity and further, if some of the tribesmen of *Taghlab* declare to become Muslims after the levy of Jiziyah, they may be allowed to do so."

(*Tabari, Vol. IV, p. 198*)

(157)

Hadrat Nu'maan bin 'Adi Sahabi (R.A.A.) was appointed revenue collector for the district of Maisaan in Lower Iraq, whose wife did not give him willingness to leave Madina for the new assignment, so Hadrat Nu'maan had to proceed to duty alone. The fertility of the soil of the district, Maisaan, and the luxuriant way of life provided there, were quite enchanting for Hadrat Nu'maan (R.A.A.), who wrote the following couplets for his wife to persuade her to come to him.

1. Is there any one who can inform my wife (in Madina) that her husband is provided wine with the glass and precious blue jugs.
2. Whenever I am in a mood to listen music, the musician on the way and the *muqqadam* of the village entertain me with their songs.
3. If the Commander of the Believers is apprised of the fact that I, along with my companions, drink in the tattered fort, surely he will get angry." The Caliph wrote the following:

"In the name of Allah, the Beneficent Most Merciful.
Ha-Mim. The revelation of the scripture from Allah, the Mighty, the Knower. The Forgiver of sin, the Accepter of repentance, the Stern in punishment, the Bountiful. (40 : 1 to 3).

The verses you wrote to your wife, one of them being No. 3 cited above was surely disliked by me. Therefore I dismiss you from office." (*Buladuri, p. 393*).

Tabaqaat Ibn-Sa'd it is stated that the Caliph in Islam, Hadrat 'Umar Farooq (R.A.A.) definitely declared his disapproval after hearing the above couplet and further declared that if any one goes to Nu'maan (R.A.A.) he should inform him (Nu'maan R.A.A.) that I (Khalifa 'Umar Farooq (R.A.A.) have removed him from office."

(*Vol. 4, p. 103*).

(158)

TO HADRAT ABU QURRAH (R.A.A.), THE QADI OF KUFA

"Some people take government money on the plea that they will go in for Jehad. But when the officer-in-authority orders them to proceed for Jehad, they put off going there and ultimately do not go at all."

(*Ibn Sa'd, Vol. VI, p. 102*)

(159)

TO HADRAT QADI SHURAIH (R.A.)

He was appointed as Qadi in 18 A.H. in Kufa and remained in his office for more than sixty years:

"If a problem comes up before you and its solution is available in the Quraan, do act accordingly without any consideration whatsoever of the opinion of any jurist. If the solution of the problem is not found in the Quraan and is to be found in the Sunnah, do it according to the Sunnah. If the solution of the problem is not to be found in the Quraan and Sunnah by you, do take the help of the opinion of the authorised, distinguished *mujtahids.* If they fail to provide any legal solution to the problem under consideration, you are entitled to exercise your power of discretion in the application of *Ijtihaad* or refer the matter to me. And my view is that it is better if you refer the case to me."

(Ibn Sa'd, Vol. VI, p. 102).

(160)

TO HADRAT QADI SHURAIH (R.A.)

Do not fight or quarrel, neither sell nor buy in the courts. When you are in anger do not pronounce judgement on any case."

(*Jaahiz, Vol. II, p. 75*).

According to some narrators the instructions provided in the above two cited letters were given orally by the Khalifa Hadrat 'Umar Farooq (R.A.A.) when the above said Qadi was proceeding to Kufa to take charge of the post. The instructions contained the following words :

"Whatever verdict you find in the Quraan act accordingly without hesitation, if it is not there, refer the case to the Sunnah of the Prophet Muhammad (S.A.W). If you are not able to find it out there, exercise your sense and power of discretion, i.e., *Ijtihaad.* Apart from this, neither fight nor quarrel in the court, neither sell nor buy within the Courts of Law."

(*Baihaqi, Vol. X, p. 110*).

(161)

TO HADRAT QADI SHURAIH (R.A.)

"There is no difference of compensation awarding in the matter of big or small teeth ; or the big and small fingers."

(*Kanzul 'Ummaal, Vol. 5, p. 16*).

(162)

TO QADI SHURAIH (R.A.)

"The child brought by the mother from the land of the enemy belligerent country to Da-rus-Salam cannot be heir to the mother, unless witnesses are produced for the testimony of his father that the child belongs to him. The testimony of the mother only is not acceptable even if she produces the child in the tattered garments of its birth."

("*Kanzul 'Ummaal Vol. 7 p. 306*).

(163)

TO HADRAT SA'D BIN ABI WAQQAS (R.A.A.)

When Yazdgard saw that the Muslim Arab forces had forced themselves into Iraq and side by side they had taken possession of the vital portion of Ahwaz; he was highly perturbed by the critical situation. He brought pressure upon his subordinate officers to do all to turn out the Arabs from their land, with the result that there was considerable zeal and fervour among the elite of Iraq and Ahwaz. Naturally, they engaged themselves in military preparations against the Muslims. The Muslim Commander-in-Chief, Harqoos bin Zuhair informed, Hadrat 'Umar Farooq (R.A.A.) about the activities of the Iranians, especially the Persian Commander of the area, Harmuzaan. He (R.A.A.) requested the Khalifa for military succour, who wrote the following urgent letter to the governor of Kufa, Hadrat Sa'd bin Abi Waqqas (R.A.A.) in response to the need of Commander of the Muslim forces in Iraq :

"Despatch immediately an army of considerable strength on the front of Ahwaz whose Commander-in-chief should be Hadrat Nu'maan bin Miqran (R.A.). Other Commanders of the force with their different contingents Jareer bin Abdullah Himyari Suwaid bin Miqran, Abdullah bin Zi Sehmeen, Jareer bin Abdullah Bajali, should march towards the headquarter of Harmuzaan and enquire about the veracity of the news regarding the breach of convenant. They should also try to find out the future plan of Harmuzaan and his intentions."

(*Tabari, Vol. IV, p. 215*).

(164)

TO HADRAT ABU MUSA ASH'ARI (R.A.A.)

The following despatch was sent to Hadrat Abu Musa Ash'ari (R.A.A.), Governor of Basra, after the above cited order in the name of Hadrat Sa'd (R.A.A.) :

'Send a formidable force to Ahwaaz under the Command of Sahl bin 'Adi brother of Suhail bin 'Adi. The undermentioned officers should accompany him as commanders of their respective contingents. Baraa bin Maalik, 'Aasim bin 'Amr, Majzaat bin Saur, Ka'b bin Saur, Urfajah bin Harsamah, Huzaifa bin Mohsin, Abdur Rehman bin Sahl, and Haseen bin Mabud. The entire force of Basra and Kufa should be under the command of Abu Sabrah bin Ruhm (R.A.A.) including the military succour that may arrive subsequently."

(*Tabari, Vol. IV, p. 215*)

(165)

TO THE FORCES IN JANDI SAABUR

The Muslim forces were concentrating upon the vital city, Jandi Saabur, the last of the cities of Ahwaaz, after conquering Ram Hermuz, Eizuj, Tustar and Soos. One of the slaves of the Muslims, on his own accord threw a Letter of Protection to the inhabitants of town by means of an arrow. Subsequently the residents of the beseiged city opened its gates wide open so that their cattle came out. The Muslims were surprised to see this state of affairs and asked the reason to open the gate of the city. They replied that the Muslims have thrown the Letter of Protection tied down to an arrow, indicating cessation of hostilities and protection of life and property after due payment of Jiziyah. The Muslims enquired about the same in their camp and subsequently it transpired that a slave in the army had done so. The elders in the forces declined to accept it as it was done by their slave without authentication. The elite of the city claimed that it was the lawful act done by the Muslim army whether he may be a slave. If they are not ready to accept the same, the elite of the city will again close the gate of the city. However the matter was referred to Hadrat 'Umar Farooq (R.A.A.) the Commander of the believers and the following was the reply :

"Allah, the Almighty, ordained high station for the fulfilment of the covenant and you can never be faithful to Allah until and unless you adhere to the execution of the promise inspite of the prevailing doubt. Whatever covenant is written in the letter of the slave that should be carried out in letter and spirit with the inhabitants of Jandi Saabur.

(*Tabari, Vol. IV, p. 231*)

There are various versions regarding the letter under reference. According to some narrators, and reporters the matter relates to the coastal city Sairaf of the province of Fars, but the contents and meanings are almost identical.

(166)

TO HADRAT SA'D BIN ABI WAQQAS (R.A.A.)

"None of the horses should be demasculated and should not be made to run more than two miles in one stretch."

(*Sarakhsi, Vol. I, p. 62*)

(167)

TO HADRAT SA'D BIN ABI WAQQAS (R.A.A.)

A Muslim looted the treasury (baitul-maal) in Kufa. The governor informed the Khalifa, who replied as under :

"The hand of the thief should not be cut off."

(*Abu Yusuf, Kitabul Kharaj, p. 171*)

(168)

TO HADRAT SA'D BIN ABI WAQQAS (R.A.A.) OR 'AMMAAR BIN YASIR (R.A.A.)

Hadrat 'Ammaar bin Yasir (R.A.A.) became the governor of Kufa after Hadrat Sa'd bin Abi Waqqas (R.A.A.)

Nahrul-mulk, a sub-division of Baghdad, was in possession of a *zimmi* woman, who subsequently embraced Islam and requested the governor to accept one-tenth of the produce (ushr) from her instead of normal land revenue on the plea that she had become a Muslim. Her plea was rejected by the Caliph on the ground that the Muslims had conquered the land by force before her acceptance of Islam, therefore, she was not entitled to the concession asked for. The reply of the Caliph was very pithy in the following words : "The land should be given to the lady and revenue should be realized."

(*Abu Yusuf, Kitabul Kharaj, p. 171*).

(169)

TO HADRAT SA'D BIN ABI WAQQAS (R.A.A.)

A sum of money remained in excees after disposing of the share of each *mujahid* from the booty, so the matter was referred to the Caliph for its further distribution. The following reply was received :

"The excess money may be handed over to the reciters of Quraan Majeed."

After the receipt of the above, two horsemen came to Hadrat Sa'd bin Abi Waqqas (R.A.A.) who were not expert in memorization of the Quraan but had rendered ycomen services in the battlefield for the cause of Islam. One of them, Bashar bin Rabiah, also composed some verses, detailing his meritorious services in the battlefield and thus expressed his desire for reward. So Hadrat Sa'd bin Abi Waqqas (R.A.A.) sought the permission of the Caliph to give the remaining amount to them, the following reply came in :

"The remainder money should be given to them in token of their meritorious war services."

(170)

From the above cited it transpires that the then government of Caliphate was inclined to appreciate the services of war veterans so Bashar sent those verses in writing to the Caliph he had composed and read out to the provincial governor. The couplets so sent to the Caliph produced the desired effect, who wrote to the governor, Sa'd bin Abi Waqqas (R.A.A.).

"Enlist Bashar bin Rabiah among the meritorious workers of ghazis. They yeomen services of the *ghazis* known (*ah-lul-balaa*) were entitled to an annual stipend of two and a half thousand *dirhams* while the general *ghazis* were receiving only two thousand.

(171)

TO HADRAT SA'D BIN ABI WAQQAS (R.A.A.)

The people of Kufa came to know that the Caliph 'Umar Farooq (R.A.A.) is in a mood to reward the reciters of Quraan Majeed, so they engaged themselves in reading the Quraan and there were more than seventy in comparison to the last year's figure of seven. So the Caliph had to revise his orders :

"The remaining excess amount may be distributed among the brave ghazis engaged in the war services in the cause Islam and particularly among those who inflicted serious injuries to the enemy."

(172)

TO HADRAT SA'D BIN ABI WAQQAS (R.A.A.)

"If you wish to know how much you are loved by Allah, try to see how much people love you. Remember, the more people are benefitted by your services, the more you will be eligible to Divine Reward."

(*Ibn 'Abd Rabbah, Vol. 2, p. 312*)

(173)

TO HADRAT SA'D BIN ABI WAQQAS (R.A.A.)

The Iranian Emperior, Yazdgird, saw with his own eyes that the Arabs have conquered Ahwaaz also and their intentions of further conquests are being constantly strengthened due to their increased activities, he managed to despatch urgent letters to the provincial governors to send army contingents, and decided to combat the Muslims from the city of Nehawand, the fortified fort of the province of Jabal where many other defensive facilities were available to him. Hadrat 'Umar Farooq (R.A.A.) was apprised of the then existing situation, who sent the following despatch to Hadrat

Sa'd bin Abi Waqqas (R.A.A.):

"Nu'maan (bin Maqran) had written to me that you have entrusted him with the task of revenue collection against his aptitude. He is saturated with the burning desire of Jehad, so you should send him as the Supreme in Command of the most vital expedition of the time, Nehawand."

(*Tabari, Vol. 4, p. 232*)

(174)

TO HADRAT NU'MAAN BIN MAQRAN (R.A.A.)

"*In the name of Allah, the Benevolent and Most Merciful.*

Salaam (Peace and Blessings of Allah) from His servant, 'Umar, the commander of the faithful. I am grateful to Almighty Allah except Whom there is none worthy of worship. It has come to my notice that the Persians had gathered a large army in Nehawand to fight against you. On receipt of this letter you may come out to fight with them with whatever Muslims are available with you on the basis of the Divine Help in Command. Neither take there Muslim Mujahids from hard rugged mountainous routes nor deprive them of their just rights, otherwise they will turn renegade form Islam: Neither should they be asked to cross jungles (where they may become ill or prey to the wild beasts). I value the life of a Muslim more than a hundred thousand *dinars.*"

(*Ibn A'sim, p. 70*)

There are many versions of the above cited despatch as mentioned in *Ibn A'sim*, *Tabari* and *Iktifa.* But the more detailed account compels one to express scepticism over its veracity, The short, pithy and the meaningful words are apt to be more exact than the lengthy discussions.

(175)

TO HADRAT NU'MAAN BIN MAQRAN (R.A.A.)

According to the narration of Saif bin 'Umar (R.A.A.) Hadrat Nu'maan, was encamping at a place known as Tarz, situated about twenty miles from Hulwaan, The army form Kufa met Hadrat Nu'maan (R.A.A.) at the above stated place, about a hundred miles from Nehawand. It was from this place that the Commander of the Nehawand expedition despatched mobile contingents under Hadrat Tulaiha, Hadrat 'Amr bin Ma'di karb and Hadrat 'Amr bin Abi Salma to know the lie of the land through circumspection. At that moment, the following memorable despatch from Amirul-mu'mineen Hadrat 'Umar Farooq (R.A.A.) was received :

"There are many persons under your command who were war-veterans influential men during the period of *Jahiliyah.* Prefer them over those who possess lesser insight in art of war-fare, consult them, act according to their advice, especially from Hadrat Tulaiha, Hadrat 'Amr bin Ma'di karb and Hadrat 'Amr bin Salma. But do not entrust them with any office in the army."

'There are many versions of the same letter in *Tabari, Aghani, Ibnul-hadid and IzaalatulKhifa* purporting to the same contents and meanings.

(176)

TO THE PERSIAN FORCES IN NEHAWAND

Hadrat Nu'maan (R.A.A.) had been ordered by the Caliph Hadrat 'Umar Farooq (R.A.A.) to invite the Persians to Islam. Further, 'Umar Farooq (R.A.A.) had addressed them direct and the following despatch was read out to the Persian forces by Mughirah bin Shu'ba (R.A.A.) on behalf of the Caliph 'Umar Farooq (R.A.A.):

"We do invite you to Islam as has been done by Allah and His Messenger, Muhammad (S.A.W.) If you respond, you are our brothers. You will be eligible to all those rights that we enjoy and shall be liable to all those responsibilities that are shared by us. If you do not want to be Muslims, be ready to pay Jiziyah. If you are not prepared to pay even Jiziyah, we will invoke Divine help of Allah, the Almighty against you.

(*Izaalatul- Khifa, Vol.II, p. 193*)

(177)

TO THE MILITARY COMMANDERS IN AHWAAZ

During the days of Hadrat 'Umar (R.A.A.), Ahwaaz enjoyed a strategical position because many routes passed through Ahwaaz for the passengers from Persia to Nehwand. So one of the basic steps taken by Hadrat 'Umar Farooq (R.A.A.) was to order the military commanders posted on the frontiers of Ahwaaz to intercept the commissariat of the Persians to Nehawand by erecting military check posts:

"Intercept the commissariat from Persia to Nehawand against your brother Muslims, thus you will be in a position to help defend your nation and the land, Remain firm on the border of Persia and Nehawand till you receive my instructions."

(*Tabari, Vol. IV, P. 239*)

(178)

TO HADRAT ABDULLAH BIN ABDULLAH BIN 'UT BAAN. (R.A.A.)

When Hadrat Sa'd bin Abi Waqqas (R.A.A.) was removed from the governorship of Kufah Ibn'Utbaan was appointed as Governor. After writing to Hadrat Nu'maan bin Maqran (R.A.A.) the following despatch was received by 'Abdullah (R.A.A.):-

"Despatch military contingents from Kufa to Hadrat Nu'maan bin Maqran. I have written'to him to march forward from Ahwaaz towards Maah (probably Maah-Shahr Yaaraan).

The army from Kufah should meet with the forces of Nu'maan (R.A.A.) and thus march towards Nehawand in a combined manner, The Commander-in-chief of the forces of Kufah shall remain Hadrat Huzaifa bin Yamaan (R.A.A.) till they join the army with Nu'maan bin Maqran. I have also written to him that per chance he encounters any particular incident, the supreme in command shall be Hadrat Huzaifa bin Yamaan (R.A.A.) In the event of his death, Hadrat Na'eem bin Maqran (R.A.A.) will replace him."

(*Tabari, Vol. IV, p. 239*)

(179)

TO HADRAT 'ABDULLAH BIN 'ABDULLAH BIN 'UTBAAN (R.A.A.)

Hurmuzaan was the Persian Governor of the province of Ahwaaz, whose southern portion of territory was conquered by the Muslims in 16 A.H. He subsequently made peace with the Muslims regarding the rest of his possessions by paying Jiziyah on their behalf. The news reached the Persian Emperor, Shah Yazdgard, who was planning at Merv to conquer the lost territories. He wrote to different governors under him to rise against the Muslims and muster up their forces to meet the Muslim enemy. Consequently the letter was also addressed to Hurmuzaan assuring him of the immediate help from all sides against the enemy. Emboldened by the encouraging letter from the Emperor of Iran, a wave of rebellion rose in Persia against the Muslims, especially the famous fortress of Tustur was a formidable scene of operations as the residents of the same beseiged themselves to offer a firm resistence to the Muslims. They created havoc in the rank and file of the Muslims. At long last, the Muslims could find out a secret way entrance into the fortress and captured it. Hurmuzan sought refuge in another fortress nearby and declared his intention to surrender provided the Caliph 'Umar Farooq (R.A.A.) decided their fate himself. The condition was accepted and a deputation along with the well-known wise man of the time, Hadrat Ahnaf bin Qais, Hurmuzaan and Khums started for Madina. The Caliph, Hadrat 'Umar Farooq (R.A.A.) apprehended that the Muslims maltreated the Persians, hence the rebellions in Ahwaaz and the consequent twice breach of covenant on the part of Hurmuzaan. So the Caliph said to the deputationists, " It seems that excesses are being committed by the Muslims against the Zimmi Persians, so they often turn hostile."

The members of the deputation replied, "So far we know, the treatment of the Muslims with the Zimmis is quite good."

Naturally Amirul-Mu'mineen 'Umar Farooq (R.A.A.) asked, "What is the reason of these rebellions?"

The sagacious, prudent Arab, Hadrat Ahnaf bin Qais (R.A.A.) gave the following answer,

"O Amirul-Mu'mineen : You have ordered not to proceed further in Persia. According to your command, we are to content ourselves with the land that has been captured so far. The real reason is that the Persian Emperor is still alive, stirring up his people, who will remain in a state of constant warfare against us as long as the Emperor is supporting them because the land is still a bone of contention between the two rulers, till one overpowers the other and the hopes of the Persians are finally frustrated as regards succour from their emperor. So the permission to advance further is the practical need of the hour. The last hopes centred in the person of their Persian Emperor, need to be eliminated for ever, so that they never think of raising heads against the Muslims any more."

Hadrat 'Umar Farooq (R.A.A.) was highly impressed by the powerful speech of Hadrat Ahnaf (R.A.A.) and declared, "Your stand seems to be correct." The proposition was still in the offing, the news came that the forces of Yazdgard had gathered themselves in Nehawand and some of them advanced towards Iraq. Whole attention of Hadrat 'Umar Farooq (R.A.A.) was concentrated to ward off this new formidable danger. A crushing defeat inflicted upon the Iranians and their emperor convinced 'Umar Farooq (R.A.A.) that action on the proposals of Hadrat Ahnaf (R.A.A.) is inevitable. After the battle of Nehawand fresh rebellions of the people of Iran in Denur and Hamdaan crept in, so the Caliph ordered the opening of four fronts against the enemy in Persia under separate commands from Kufa and Basra. It was in connection with the seige of Isfahaan that the Caliph, 'Umar Farooq (R.A.A.), wrote to Hadrat Ibn 'Utbaan (R.A.A.):

"March off from Kufa towards Madaain and invite the Muslims to participate in the Jehad and inform me of the situation existing there including those who voluntarily agree to take part in the fight as a result of declared Jihad".

(*Tabari, Vol. IV, p. 246*)

(180)

TO HADRAT SAA'IB BIN AQRA' (R.A.A.)

After the conquest of Nehawand, Saa'ib (R.A.A.) was appointed collector of taxes in the capital of Iraq, Madain. During this period there was rebellion in Hamadan and Jalula. The rebels caught hold the resident Arabs and their slaves. Some of them were sold out in the open market and the rest were kept under their personal use. Some of the slaves including their Arab masters were taken out from the possession of the rebels, but the matter was referred to the Khalifa regarding the rest of the Arabs and their slaves, who were sold out in the market as to how they should be acquired whether by force or through payment of price. The following reply was received :

"Those Muslims who could find their articles intact should be handed over to them, but that which has become the property of the merchants can not be taken back except through payment of the original price paid for the free Arabs as a free person can neither be sold nor purchased."

(*Kanzul-'Ummal, Vol. II p. 313*)

(181)

TO HADRAT ABU MUSA ASH'ARI (R.A.A.)

There is extreme type of versions regarding the conquest of the Province of Ahwaaz i.e. (Khuzistan) by Hadrat Abu Musa 'Ash'ari (R.A.A.). In this connection it is unnecessary to enter into the labyrinth of the details of the views of different historians, who give full credit to Hadrat Abu Musa Ash'ari (R.A.A.) for the conquest of the entire province of Ahwaaz. The fact is that there is no limit to human achievement provided one does not care who gets the credit. However, we reproduce the following English version of the letter whose contents were addressed to Abu Musa Ash'ari (R.A.A.) by the Caliph, Hadrat 'Umar Farooq (R.A.A.):

"*In the Name of Allah, the Compassionate and Most Merciful.*

Let it be perfectly clear and known to Abdullah bin Qais i.e. Abu Musa 'Ash'ari on behalf of 'Abdullah 'Umar bin Khattab that the Persians have mustered their forces in Ahwaaz,Tastur, Manazir and other adjoining areas. They are ready to attack the Muslims. Immediately on receipt of this letter and knowing its contents, you should raise a huge army. Be consisderate to the people of Basra, especially to those who desire to go and join the Muslim forces that should be upto the maximum as far as possible. March on to fight till you reach the enemy territory — the first thing to be done without fear of contradiction and consultation is to invite the people to *Deen-e-Haq* (the True Way of Islam) and whoso accepts the invitation and the Call, grant him full protection of life, property and honour, availing of his assets upto the minimum of your needs during exigency. Do continue to plead to yourself to be on the Right Way of life as far as possible. Do not engage the *ghazis* or fighters in the way of Allah to the extent that they feel disgusted and are tired of the engagement as they are required to participate in the battle with true zeal and spirit. Treat all nicely and be modest. Remember none can attain that height of glory among the created creatures of Allah whose record is free from the excesses committed. Ensure justice to the grieved and the unjust must pay the due of the grieved person. Try to engender friendship and uniformity of action among the Muslims, exhort them to read the Quraan and be fearful of the Divine chastisement, keep away people to dilate upon the stories of the period of Ignorance (Jahiliyah) because the way of the Jahiliyah or ignorance will create heart-burning and malice among the people and the old enemities will be revived. O Son of Qais (Abu Musa 'Ash'ari R.A.A.) remember that Allah has taken upon Himself the promise of victory for the true believers in Islam. So be steadfast in your life so that Allah may be pleased with you lest He may divert His attention of Grace from you and another nation may become entitled to this Grace and Mercy of Allah instead of you."

(Ibn A'sim, p. 63)

(182)

TO HADRAT ABU MUSA ASH'ARI (R.A.A.) AND THE ARMY

On receipt of the above cited letter Hadrat Abu Musa Ash'ari (R.A.A.) marched towards Ahwaaz with an army from Basra whose encounter took place with the Juts and the Asawaris. They fought valiantly but ultimate discomfiture was their doom. The Juts were mainly the tillers of the soil and the Asawaris were the landlords, both of whom were enslaved by the Muslims. Naturally, the question arose about the cultivation and looking after the land. Hadrat 'Umar Farooq (R.A.A.) was apprised of the exact local situation in the matter, who wrote the following :

"Cultivation and agriculture is beyond your control, so leave it to their cultivators, free the slaves and realize land revenue from them."

(183)

TO HADRAT ABU MUSA ASH'ARI (R.A.A.) AND THE ARMED FORCES OF ISLAM

After settling the matter with the Juts and the Asawaris, Hadrat Abu Musa Ash'ari marched towards Manazir, the important city of Ahwaaz. The same, was subdued with the use of sword, whose inhabitants were identical with the people of Ahwaaz. So the same conditions were applied and the Caliph, 'Umar Farooq (R.A.A.) replied as under :

"No doubt Manazir is like an adjoining locality of Iraq, so give back whatever has been found there."

(*Buladuri, p. 385*)

(184)

TO HADRAT ABU MUSA ASH'ARI (R.A.A.)

The Muslims captured many strong, sturdy black horses of Iraq like those of the Arabs, so Hadrat Abu Musa Ash'ari wrote for advice regarding thier disposal as booty. The following reply from the Khalifa was received:

"These horses are of Turkish origin: who so performs duty like Arab horses that should be given one share from the booty, the rest should be given nothing."

(*Sarakhsi, Vol. II, p. 179*)

(185)

TO HADRAT ABU MUSA ASH'ARI

In fact, the Asawaris were convinced of the bravery and devotion of Muslim soldiers, so their leader, Sherooyah Aswari, entered into an alliance with the Muslims on the condition that the following terms shall be ratified by the Khalifa to enable them to enter the fold of Islam :

(1) They will fight against the Persians in collaboration with the Muslims.

(2) Observe strict neutrality when the Muslims differ in themselves.

(3) If an Arab fights with them, the Muslims shall help the Asawaris.

(4) Shall be rehabilitated in the city of our choice.

(5) Shall join any tribe of their choice.

(6) Should be granted distinction in honour and stipend

(7) Finally the Khalifa in Islam should sign the covenant.

Hadrat Abu Musa 'Ash'ari (R.A.A.) sent the above stipulations to the Khalifa, Hadrat 'Umar Farooq (R.A.A.) for ratification. All their demands were accepted. They started taking part in the seige of Tastur but did not show the courage and fighting skill expected of them under their leader, Siyah. Abu Musa 'Ash'ari (R.A.A.) complained about the same to their leader, who replied that they were new converts in Islam and as such they were lacking the fervour and zeal of the old devout Muslims. Moreover, they had not so far been provided with the promised distinguished stipends of distinction and honour. The matter was reported to the Khalifa who replied as under :

"The officers of the royal army should be awarded distinction in honour and money according to their conduct in the battle as is granted to an Arab."

(*Tabari, Vol. IV, p. 218*).

(186)

TO ABU MUSA ASH'ARI (R.A.A.)

After the conquest of Soos, the Muslims entered the fortress and found a corpse of a dead person wrapped in zarbaft (a costly cloth duly interwoven with gold fibre), a huge amount of money with a writing that who needed money could take it on loan for a fixed period and must return the same during the stipulated time otherwise the defaulter shall be a victim of leprosy. After due enquiry it was ascertained that the dead body was of Prophet Daniyal, who was brought from Iraq (Babul) to Soos on the assurance of the people because they believed that due rain could be had through his blessings. Hadrat Abu Musa Ash'ari (R.A.A.) sought instructions from the Khalifa 'Umar Farooq (R.A.A.), to dispose of the body and the money. The following is the reply:

"The corpse should be enwrapped in the Coffin, duly scented, prayed for, buried like other Prophets and money deposited in the State treasury."

(*Kanzul 'Ummal, Vol. VI, p. 310*)

(187)

TO HADRAT ABU MUSA ASH'ARI (R.A.A.)

The son of an Arab, Haska by name, died, whose two relations, father and grand-mother were alive at the time of his death. Hadrat Abu Musa Ash'ari (R.A.A.) referred the matter to the Caliph 'Umar Farooq (R.A.A.) regarding their share in the heritage. The following was the reply:

"The father of Haska and the grand-mother should be given share from the heritage."

(*Kanzul-'Ummal, Vol. VI, p. 8*).

(188)

The provincial governor, Abu Musa Ash'ari (R.A.A.) further informed the Khalifa 'Umar Farooq (R.A.A.), that many people die here in the area without leaving their blood relations or even muwali i.e., the freed slaves, so he should be apprised of the practice of disposing of their heritage. The Khalifa replied as under

If a blood relative or the freed slave of the deceased is alive, he is entitled to the heritage of the person concerned: if they are not alive this heritage should be deposited as state property."

(*Kanzul-'Ummaal, Vol. IV, p. 18*)

(189)

TO HADRAT ABU MUSA ASH'ARI (R.A.A.)

"In the matter of inheritance, the grand-father should be treated at par in the absence of father. This was also practised by Sydena Hadrat Abu Bakr Siddiq (R.A.A.)."

(*Kanzul-'Ummaal, Vol. VI, p. 16*)

(190)

TO THE MEMBERS OF THE MILITARY INQUIRY COMMITTEE

Hadrat Abu Musa Ash'ari (R.A.A.) complained against the aggressive action of Hadrat Jareer bin 'Abdullah in the matter of conquest of Tustar, so the Khalifa appointed a committee of the high ranking military officers to enquire into the excesses, if any, and wrote the following :

"The matter should be looked into whether Abu Musa Ash'ari (as he claims) granted extension of six months to the people of Ramburmz or not for surrender. Whether any treaty was executed in this regard. Abu Musa Ash'ari should also be asked on solemn affirmation about it. If he affirms the same, all the slaves and girl concubines should be given back. If any woman became pregnant due to the intercourse of a Muslim, she should be detained till she gives birth to a child: afterwards she is entitled to go to Ramburmz or may live as a Muslim."

(*Nasikhut-Tawarikh, Vol. II, p. 304*)

(191)

TO HADRAT ABU MUSA ASH'ARI (R.A.A.)

The fortress of Tustar was situated on a rocky place and was surrounded by the river on two sides. A Persian informed the Muslims of the secret river route leading to fortress. Subsequently the Muslims entered the fortress by force and a huge number of pregnant women fell into their hands. The Khalifa Hadrat 'Umar Farooq (R.A.A.), came to know this and hence wrote the following :

"No Muslim should enter into conjugal relation with a pregnant woman till she gives birth to a child. The Muslims should not be the partners of the issue of the polytheists as a single drop of seed leads to the making of the child."

(*Izalatul-Khifa, Vol. II, p. 115*)

(192)

TO THE CONQUERORS OF TUSTAR

There was a difference of opinion among the forces of Basra and the army of Kufah that subsequently participated in the battle that ensured for the conquest of Tustar. Both the forces of Basra and Kufah claimed dominance in the realization of revenue and administration. The matter was referred to the Khalifa. The following reply was the answer to the problem :

"The factual position is that the army from Kufa assisted the forces of Basra and the conquest was made easy. In spite of this the real conquerors of Tustar is the Basra Army. The Muslims who are, in fact, brothers among themselves obtained victory by mutual co-operation but the real conqueror of Tustar shall be the Basra Army and the forces from Kufah shall be equally entitled to reap the benefits of booty. Both the armies should be considerate to each other and may not fight amongst themselves. Peace and Blessings of Allah be upon you."

(*Ibn A'sim, p. 67*).

* * * * * * * * * * * * * *

(Futuhul Buldan, Vol. II, p. 127)

[182]

(Tabari, Vol. [illegible], p. 675)

* * * * * * * * * *